Routledge Revivals

The Moral and Physical Condition of the Working Classes

The Moral and Physical Condition of the Working Classes

Employed in the Cotton Manufacture of Manchester

James Phillips Kay Shuttleworth

Second Edition

Routledge
Taylor & Francis Group
Routledge Revivals

First published in 1970 by Frank Cass & Co. Ltd.

This edition first published in 2018 by Routledge
2 Park Square, Milton Park, Abingdon, Oxon, OX14 4RN
and by Routledge
52 Vanderbilt Avenue, New York, NY 10017, USA

Routledge is an imprint of the Taylor & Francis Group, an informa business

Publisher's Note
The publisher has gone to great lengths to ensure the quality of this reprint but points out that some imperfections in the original copies may be apparent.

Disclaimer
The publisher has made every effort to trace copyright holders and welcomes correspondence from those they have been unable to contact.

A Library of Congress record exists under ISBN:

ISBN 13: 978-0-367-14982-6 (hbk)
ISBN 13: 978-0-367-14985-7 (pbk)
ISBN 13: 978-0-429-05428-0 (ebk)

CASS LIBRARY OF VICTORIAN TIMES

No. 4

General Editor: Anne Humpherys
Herbert H. Lehman College, New York

THE

MORAL AND PHYSICAL CONDITION

OF THE

WORKING CLASSES

THE

MORAL AND PHYSICAL CONDITION

OF THE

WORKING CLASSES

Employed in the Cotton Manufacture in Manchester

SECOND EDITION ENLARGED

And Containing an Introductory Letter
to the
REV. THOMAS CHALMERS, D.D.

BY

James Phillips Kay Shuttleworth

With a new Preface by Dr. W. H. Chaloner

FRANK CASS & CO. LTD,

1970

Published by
FRANK CASS AND COMPANY LIMITED
67 Great Russell Street, London WC1

First edition	1832
Second edition	1832
New impression of the Second edition	1970

ISBN 0 7146 2425 X

*Printed in Great Britain by Clarke, Doble & Brendon Ltd.
Plymouth and London*

PREFACE

Dr. James Phillips Kay, (later Sir James Kay-Shuttleworth) was born in Rochdale, Lancashire, in 1804, and came from a prosperous middle-class family with banking connections. After some hesitation about the choice of a career he began to study medicine at Edinburgh University in 1824 and graduated M.D. there in 1827. He then began practice in Manchester and was appointed medical officer to the Ancoats and Ardwick dispensary. In Manchester he acquired a wide knowledge of working-class conditions and diseases. In 1831–32 he acted as secretary to the Manchester Board of Health which had been set up to combat the threatened cholera epidemic. His vividly written pamphlet *The Moral and Physical Condition of the Working Classes employed in the Cotton Manufacture in Manchester* (1832) embodies the fruits of his experiences in the capital of the cotton kingdom. It is the best known of all the literature produced about the cholera epidemic and has been widely quoted by historians of economic and social conditions. It should however be noted that, thanks in part to the devoted labours of Kay and his colleagues, the cholera epidemic in Manchester proved to be relatively less severe than in cities such as Liverpool and Newcastle-upon-Tyne, which were not products of the Industrial Revolution. Francis Place considered that Kay's pamphlet should be used with caution, and believed that, despite the rapid growth of Manchester, living conditions there had improved within living memory:

"... I believe that what he (Kay) says is correct; but he gives the matter as it now stands, knowing

> nothing of former times; his picture is a very deplorable one . . . many Manchester operatives . . . inform me that his narration relates almost entirely to the state of the Irish, but that the condition of a vast number of the people was as bad some years ago, as he describes the worst portion of them to be now."[1]

After 1832 Kay led a busy life. He served for a time as an assistant poor law commissioner under the Act of 1834 (he was a friend of both Edwin Chadwick and E. C. Tufnell) and in 1839 was appointed secretary to the newly-created Committee of the Privy Council on Education, a post which he held for ten years. He is therefore one of the founders of the modern English system of public education. In 1842 he married an heiress with good expectations, Janet Shuttleworth, of Gawthorpe Hall, Lancashire, and on his marriage assumed the name of Kay-Shuttleworth. He was knighted in 1850, and played a prominent part in organising the relief of distress among the operatives during the Lancashire cotton famine of 1861–65. A Liberal in politics, he showed great interest in the problems of the mid-Victorian trade union movement, maintained a life-long interest in questions of industrial and social policy, and wrote two historical novels on Lancashire and Yorkshire themes. He died on May 26 1877 at 68 Cromwell Road, Kensington.

November 1969 W.H.C.

---

[1]Parliamentary Papers, 1835, no. 465, Vol. VII, p.838.

THE

MORAL AND PHYSICAL CONDITION

OF THE

WORKING CLASSES

EMPLOYED IN THE COTTON MANUFACTURE IN MANCHESTER.

SECOND EDITION ENLARGED:

AND CONTAINING AN INTRODUCTORY LETTER

TO THE

REV. THOMAS CHALMERS, D. D.

PROFESSOR OF DIVINITY IN THE UNIVERSITY OF EDINBURGH, ETC.

BY

JAMES PHILLIPS KAY, M. D.

LONDON:

JAMES RIDGWAY, NO. 169, PICCADILLY.

MDCCCXXXII.

TO THE

REV. THOMAS CHALMERS, D. D.

MY DEAR SIR,

THAT the former edition of this Pamphlet should have been commended by those, who, deeply conscious of the moral and physical evils endured by the working classes, earnestly seek to arouse the power and intelligence of society, to vigorous efforts for the improvement of their condition, has strengthened the strong convictions which I then felt concerning the source and the proper remedies of these ills. I was especially deeply gratified when the principles which I had there supported received the warm approbation which you so cordially expressed, since I knew that the energies of your exalted mind had long been perseveringly devoted to an investigation of the actual condition of the poor, and to a profound consideration of the means of their relief.

I have for some time delayed publishing a second edition of this pamphlet, chiefly because new sources of information have been opened to me whilst engaged with the very intelligent members of the Board of Health, established in Manchester, in devising, and urging into operation, plans for the relief of persons suffering from Cholera.

In minutely tracking the steps of this singular malady, some general considerations have been impressed upon my mind, which, as to no one can they be so appropriately offered as to yourself, so am I urged by every impulse of esteem and admiration to address them to you.

Thus occupied in tracing the means by which the contagious principle of cholera is disseminated, I have felt surprise at the singular frequency with which I have been led to the most loathsome haunts of poverty and vice. Predisposition to the reception of this contagion is strongly promoted by all those agencies which depress the physical energies: but though I was well aware of this law, I was by no means prepared to discover, that, in its operation, it observed so strict a relation to the degree in which these agencies were combined. Had I been a stranger to the purlieus of pauperism—if it had not been my custom, in the exercise of public professional duties and for purposes of local observation and inquiry, to frequent the precincts of vice and disease, thither I should have been infallibly led by this unerring guide. I am aware that exceptions to the rule have occurred elsewhere, which, as I have not witnessed them, I am not prepared to explain; but I felt a melancholy pleasure in proving the singular constancy with which this law operated here. Moreover, though I had attributed to these sources that physical depression which favours the invasion of disease, and particularly the spread of contagion, and had, ere Cholera appeared in Manchester, predicated its haunts, yet this practical demonstration of a theoretical law did not fail to produce in my mind the effect of a deeper and more entire conviction of the amount and quality of the evils flowing from these sources, and a more eager determination to attempt their removal.

You, who minister in the sacred office, must have more frequent opportunities than I, of observing with regret, that many who recognize the constant presence of a presiding Providence, fail in practically acknowledging the perpetual influence of a mighty source of moral causation; and especially, that they witness great events rather with the ignorant wonder of the savage, than with that enlightened sagacity, which seeks, with humility and caution, to discover their great moral tendencies. You must have perceived that such men regard great epochs, such as a pestilence or a famine, as isolated facts of history, as though eras which powerfully affect the human mind, could possibly be separated from their inevitable moral consequences, and hence from those events which necessarily flow from them. Nay, it is astonishing that they do not perceive, that it is utterly impossible to separate any event which is witnessed by a human intelligence, from a certain inevitable moral sequence; or that they who know that to drop a pebble on the surface of the world disturbs the planet, should not perceive how, of an equal necessity, events acting on the human spirit, in proportion to their novelty and power, disturb, for good or for ill, the constitution of society.

These observations premised, you will pardon me, if, having been placed constantly in the presence of that malady which has ravaged our country, and having been engaged in minutely contemplating its progress, I should presume upon that acquaintance with its operation which I have reaped by study, so far, as to indicate certain *moral consequences*, which it seems likely to induce in the class amongst which it prevails, and amongst the other orders of society.

It is melancholy to perceive, how many of the evils suffered by the poor flow from their own ignorance or moral errors. In a much worse state of society, sobriety, prudence, industry, and forethought, would produce more real comfort, not to speak of domestic happiness and that inward quiet which flows from a well founded self respect, than would the greatest external prosperity, in which ignorance, dissolute habits, imprudence and idle extravagance prevailed. Some prejudiced men, accustomed to examine only one side of the shield, are hence eager to attribute all the evils suffered by the poor, solely to their ignorance or moral deviations. On the contrary, not only do they suffer under the pressure of extraneous grievances, but even those which immediately flow from their own habits, may often be traced to the primary influence of the imperfect institutions of society on their character—to the combined effects of an untutored ignorance—bad example, uncounteracted by a system of moral instruction—and the desperate straits of a perverted spirit battling with hunger and toil. Their errors are not more their fault than their misfortune, and they, who would rescue them from their condition, must depend not alone on elevating them physically, but must seek to produce a strong and permanent moral impression. In these efforts the disease now prevailing in their habitations, and likely, I fear, to remain as an endemic malady, is powerfully calculated to assist, as it conveys the strongest admonition of the consequences of insobriety, uncleanliness, and that improvidence and idleness which waste the comforts of life, induce weakness, and invite disease.

Especially in the present state of society, persevering industry, watchful forethought, scrupulous temperance and economy are necessary to elevate a working man into a situation of physical comfort, and abundant means may be speedily dissipated in the absence of these presiding virtues of poverty. A well furnished habitation in a salubrious site, nutritious food, decent comforts, and warm clothing, may speedily be exchanged, by the tavern spendthrift for a narrow ill ventilated apartment, rickety furniture scarcely capable of sustaining his squalid family, whilst he, his character lost, may roam in ragged beggary, in vain seeking the means of sustenance, and return to the noisome court and thickly peopled barrack of pauperism in which is his abode, conveying in his own bosom from some haunt of vice, the fatal element of contagion to poison his offspring. On the other hand, he that would extricate his family from the loathsome dwelling in the close alley, amongst whose debased inhabitants cholera lurks, and would seek some more salubrious abode, and would even then banish the enemy from his household, must provide the means of sustaining it in a state of physical comfort, lest, when he is least aware, it desolate his home.

This is a theme whose practical comment is unfortunately at every door, and on which we are anxious to invite every well wisher to the poor to enlarge. From events happening in the vicinity of their dwellings, which demonstrate that the fatal visitations of Cholera are made in the houses of squalid poverty and reckless vice, they will not fail to draw arguments in favour of industry and virtue, if care be taken that they substitute none of that vulgar sophistry which ignorance suggests to delude. One thing is necessary, *that the impressions, which the events are themselves calculated to make, should be sedulously strengthened by earnest admonitions, from every source of public ministration and of private counsel.*

On the other orders of society, Cholera commits such occasional inroads, that if those sympathies which attach us to all our kind were in no respect outraged, and man,—individuality lost in the impersonated generality,—did not stand forth to resist his invisible enemy, still selfishness would prompt those elevated above poverty anxiously to watch the insidious progress of a malady whose presence benumbs the energies of society, and paralyses commerce. He that values the precious jewel of his life, and would guard the treasure, endeavours the extirpation of a disease which like a thief walking in darkness, might, he fears, pass his threshold secretly, and rifle the casket as he sleeps.

No event is more calculated painfully to excite the public mind, than the invasion of pestilence, and since it cannot be regarded as an isolated calamity, but prevails in consequence of, and in proportion to the existence of others,—no other can be so well calculated to unmask the deformity of evils which have preyed upon the energies of the community. He whose duty it is to follow the steps of this messenger of death, must descend to the abodes of poverty, must frequent the close alleys, the crowded courts, the overpeopled habitations of wretchedness, where pauperism and disease congregate round the source of social discontent and political disorder in the centre of our large towns, and behold with alarm, in the hot-bed of pestilence, ills that fester in secret, at the very heart of society.

That these evils should have been overlooked by the aristocracy of the country, cannot excite surprise. Very few of their order reside in, or near our large provincial towns. Their visits to the country are generally intervals, snatched from the pleasures or business of the metropolis, in which their time is spent in an unbroken quiet, gentle amusements, or the unembarrassed society of a circle of friends, with some necessary attention to their estates, and the magisterial duties of a rural district. Their parks are not often traversed by those who are capable of being the exponents of the evils endured by the working classes of large towns, and the hoarse voice of popular discontent disturbs not the Arcadian stillness of the scene. No transient visit, prompted by curiosity concerning the wonderful combinations of mechanical skill, can afford them any correct knowledge of the moral and physical condition of the poor. Too often is it the interest of some to deceive them. What wonder then, that the miseries of the people have been solemnly denied in both houses of parliament—that popular tumults have been attributed, most unphilosophically (as to a sole and sufficient cause) to the instigation of unprincipled leaders,—as though a happy people could love discord —and that they who have asserted the truth have been supposed to garble facts for their own political designs. The public welfare will be most powerfully promoted by every event, which exposes the condition of the people to the gentry of England.

It might be apprehended that the merchants of the country were sufficiently conversant with the habits and wants of the operative population. The pure merchant is, however, seldom in immediate contact with the people. No association exists between him and them—the scenes of his enterprise are distant, and the objects of his calculation concern not the methods of production, but the barter of things produced. The productive classes of society are engaged in supplying the elements of commercial exchange, but he only in effecting the exchange itself. The ingenuity, the minute knowledge of detail, and the industry expended in the execution of his plans, suppose so complete an absorption of the whole intellectual capacity, that we can scarcely wonder that few engaged in the anxious and harassing pursuits of commerce, should find leisure to become personally acquainted with the state of the population, much less to expose the evils which they suffer.

Between the manufacturers of the country, staggering under the burdens of an enormous taxation and a restricted commerce; between them and the labouring classes subjects of controversy have arisen, and consequent animosity too generally exists. The burdens of trade diminish the profits of capital, and the wages of labour: but bitter debate arises between the manufacturers and those in their employ, concerning the proper division of that fund, from which these are derived. The bargain for the wages of labour develops organized associations of the working classes, for the purpose of carrying on the contest with the capitalist: large funds are subscribed: frequent meetings are held, at which inflammatory harangues are delivered, and committees and delegates chosen;—a gloomy spirit of discontent is engendered, and the public are not unfrequently alarmed, by the wild out-break of popular violence, when mobs of machine breakers defy the armed guardians of the peace. In these contests personal animosity and party rancour have sometimes indulged in the most flagrant excesses; the characters of individuals have been most grossly maligned, their property destroyed, and such severe personal assaults have been made on those of the labouring class, who did not unite in the general league, that they have occasionally produced the loss of life, and, more than once, a master has been sacrificed by an assassin.

Notwithstanding these demonstrations of insensate rage, the enlightened manufacturers of the country, acutely sensible of the miseries of large masses of the operative body, are to be ranked amongst the foremost advocates of every measure which can remove the pressure of the public burdens from the people, and the most active promoters of every plan which can conduce to their physical improvement, or their moral elevation. There are, it is to be lamented, a few who would hide the condition of the working classes, lest its exposure should become an apology for the excesses of the operatives, or an argument in favour of the nostrums of political speculators. When this results not from ignorance it is a crime, and I am not willing to screen those from just contempt, who are so blind to the true interests of their own order, or so fearful of the propositions of every quack, that, deaf to the appeals of humanity, they represent the people to be happy and contented. Surely, if they are stubborn to the threats and furious assaults of the enraged populace, still the scenes of suffering which they behold, the embarrassments of their own enterprises, and the expostulations of the wise, might dissuade them from pursuing the crooked schemes of a narrow and devious policy.

Notwithstanding the general knowledge which the manufacturers must have of the condition of the working classes, yet, before the appearance of the Cholera, they were not so well convinced as they now are, that the minute personal interference of the higher ranks is necessary to the physical and moral elevation of the poor. A new sphere is now opened, to which their personal safety attracts their attention, and in which the most active benevolence may expand and exhaust itself. The pestilence is in their cities—at their very doors—daily it smites in the crowded manufactories, and snatches its victims from their very side. All past schemes—all past exertions have been futile: some new development of merciful interference, is necessary to raise the people above the influence of a new disease. In this spirit, in anticipation of the invasion of Cholera, the inspections of the streets and houses of the large towns, were performed with a zeal and energy, which proved how powerfully the sympathies and anxieties of the inhabitants were awakened.

The dense masses of the habitations of the poor, which stretch out their arms, as though to grasp and enclose the dwellings of the noble and wealthy, in the metropolis, and in our large provincial cities, have heretofore been regarded as mighty wildernesses of building, in which the incurable ills of society rankled, beyond the reach of sanative interference. The good despaired that by their individual efforts they could relieve the miseries, which, in their errands of mercy, they beheld; and committees of inquiry sat only to lengthen the records of crime, mendicity, ignorance and pauperism. One fact alone became prominent, *that the united exertions of the individual members of society were required, to procure a moral and physical change in the community;* and it was evident that some circumstance was wanting, to disturb the apathy which paralysed their energies.

The ingression of a disease, which threatens, with a stealthy step, to invade the sanctity of the domestic circle; which may be unconsciously conveyed from those haunts of beggary where it is rife, into the most still and secluded retreat of refinement—whose entrance, wealth cannot absolutely bar, and luxury invites, this is an event which, in the secret pang that it awakens, at the heart of all those who are bound to any others by sympathies which it may harshly rend, ensures that the anxious attention of every order of society shall be directed to that, in which social ills abound. Though the political safety of the wealthy is truly endangered when ignorance and immorality prevail amongst the poor, that fact is not rendered so apparent by daily and hourly illustration, as is the personal hazard, incurred by permitting municipal evils and barbarous manners to exist so generally as to invite the inroads, and encourage the progress of pestilence. This danger would certainly assume a more threatening aspect, were the vulgar notion removed that Cholera is a mere epidemic visitation of a few months, and were it known that once introduced, the disease generally continues to lurk long in the places where it has appeared, still desolating the community, like the plague, with occasional bursts of epidemic violence. Cholera can only be eradicated by raising the physical and moral condition of the community, in such a degree as to remove the predisposition to its reception and propagation, which is created by poverty and immorality. Were this notion, as it ought to be, widely diffused; did it become, as it will, the conviction of every intelligent man, what additional force would be added to the arguments suggested by sympathy and selfishness!

You must perceive how the constant presence of this new danger will eventually affect the public mind. Boards of Health established in conformity with the Orders in Council, will become permanent organized centres of medical police, where municipal powers will be directed by scientific men, to the removal of those agencies which most powerfully depress the physical condition of the inhabitants. But I chiefly depend on the strong impression made upon *the public mind,* when I confidently expect that the singular energy of this restless era will be directed to promote, not only by general enactment, but by individual exertion, every scheme devised for the moral elevation of the working classes.

This expectation will not be blighted, since every event combines to prove that we have arrived at a great moral and political crisis. The object of government is universally acknowledged to be the happiness of the many; and every interest is staked upon its right administration. The lives, the fortunes, and the liberties of the people will henceforth we may hope be entrusted to those who know their wants, sympathize with their distresses, and in whose experience, ability, and integrity, they can repose the trust of devising means for their relief. At this period therefore, an event which exposes the miseries and privations of the labouring classes, cannot fail to produce auspicious results.

These are some of those moral consequences which will, I conceive, flow from the introduction of Cholera.

You will not, I hope, think I am presumptuous, if I add that I am the more prone to this view of the subject, since it seems to me to afford a beautiful proof how mercy abounds even in the midst of apparent judgment. That our intellectual errors necessarily lead to mischievous consequences, and that our moral deviations are the very gates of suffering, are facts, which he that examines his inward consciousness, will find proved by daily experience. That these are the fruitful sources of the misery of the world, its whole history proclaims. Our own hands sow the seeds of evil, and we reap its harvest. But in the terrific visitations of these natural ills, whose mighty sum has been accumulated by the repeated intellectual and moral errors of man, how grateful is it to watch the constant interference of a preservative Power, whose presence pervades the world.

Signal eras of calamity are calculated to produce such deep and lasting impressions, that it is of the utmost consequence they should be rightly understood. Events attended with physical misery often create moral happiness; rouse the human spirit from apathy, and purge it from vice. Revolutions which overthrow every social institution, and dissolve every moral tie, tend by a destructive process to eradicate antiquated errors, and to reform and renovate the fabric of society. As storms dissipate pestilential miasmata, so war, the scourge of the earth, overthrows the altars of superstition, and at its very shrine immolates its priests. War, that wastes the treasures of despotism, nerves the arms of the people, and amidst the struggles of feudal pride they assert their rights, and claim their peaceful possessions. Thus it is, that the noxious elements which threaten man with physical and moral evil are dissipated, and if we are tempted to regard the ministers of a beneficent Providence as clothed in the apparel of wrath, a moment's inspection will show, that calamity is the consequence of error, but that they are messengers of mercy who bring good out of ill.

I am thus disposed to hope that many events have concurred to impress the public mind with a sense of the importance of minutely investigating the state of the working classes. Wishing to strengthen this conviction, and to assist in the benevolent designs in which it must issue, I offer the statistical evidence contained in this pamphlet, as a humble contribution to the fund of information concerning the moral and physical condition of the poor, throughout the kingdom. I have carefully avoided instituting any comparison between the state of the labouring classes of Manchester, and that of those in other large manufacturing towns. I am not without the hope that similar inquiries will be undertaken elsewhere; and if they become general, the first object of this work will be accomplished. Were such investigations conducted, with a zeal corresponding with that evinced by my fellow townsmen, in the prosecution of this, I fear it would be discovered, that Manchester might be very favourably compared with many large towns. The improvements which are constantly projected here, are carried on with an energy which shows that the inhabitants of Manchester, as they are second to none in the successful application of science to the arts—in foreign enterprise—and in wealth—so are they determined, in the future, to yield the palm to none in the perfection of their municipal regulations—the number of their institutions for the spread of knowledge and the advancement of science—in the stability of their civic economy, and the ornaments of their social state.

The evils here unreservedly exposed, so far from being the necessary consequences of the manufacturing system, have a remote and accidental origin, and might, by *judicious management*, be entirely removed. Nor do they flow from any single source: and especially in the present state of trade, the hours of labour cannot be materially diminished, without occasioning the most serious commercial embarrassment. This pamphlet chiefly exhibits a frightful picture of the effects of injudicious legislation. The evils of restricted commerce affect not the capitalist alone: for the working classes are reserved the bitterest dregs of the poisoned chalice. We have a poor law operating as a direct bounty on the increase of an indigent population—depriving the virtuous poor of the incentives to industry, and glutting the market with labour. The state receives support from taxes so regulated by recent laws, that they facilitate the increase of the haunts of intemperance, and the consequent demoralization of the people. There is no sufficient provision for the education and the religious and moral instruction of the poor; and their ignorance and misery often prompt them to desperate deeds.

These and other evils demand immediate legislative interference; and if the slight sketch contained in this pamphlet of the monstrous effects of this imperfection of the law, hasten, by one moment, the period at which that change shall be commenced, the ultimate design of its author will have been fulfilled.

I am

With great respect,

Yours,

JAMES PHILLIPS KAY.

MORAL AND PHYSICAL

CONDITION

OF THE WORKING CLASSES,

&c.

SELF-KNOWLEDGE, inculcated by the maxim of the ancient philosopher, is a precept not less appropriate to societies than to individuals. The physical and moral evils by which we are personally surrounded, may be more easily avoided when we are distinctly conscious of their existence; and the virtue and health of society may be preserved, with less difficulty, when we are acquainted with the sources of its errors and diseases.

The sensorium of the animal structure, to which converge the sensibilities of each organ, is endowed with a consciousness of every change in the sensations to which each member is liable; and few diseases are so subtle as to escape its delicate perceptive power. Pain thus reveals to us the existence of evils, which, unless arrested in their progress, might insidiously invade the sources of vital action.

Society were well preserved, did a similar faculty preside, with an equal sensibility, over its constitution; making every order immediately conscious of the evils affecting any portion of the general mass, and thus rendering their removal equally necessary for the immediate ease, as it is for the ultimate welfare of the whole social system. The mutual dependance of the individual members of society and of its various orders, for the supply of their necessities and the gratification of their desires, is acknowledged, and it imperfectly compensates for the want of a faculty, resembling that pervading consciousness which presides over the animal economy. But a knowledge of the moral and physical evils oppressing one order of the community, is by these means slowly communicated to those which are remote; and general efforts are seldom made for the relief of partial ills, until they threaten to convulse the whole social constitution.

Some governments have attempted to obtain, by specific measures, that knowledge for the acquisition of which there is no natural faculty. The statistical investigations of Prussia, of the Netherlands, of Sweden, and of France, concerning population, labour, and its commercial and agricultural results; the existing resources of the country, its taxation, finance, &c. are minute and accurate. The economist may, however, still regret, that many most interesting subjects of inquiry are neglected, and that the reports of these governments fail to give a perfect portraiture of the features of each individual part of the social body. Their system, imperfect though it be, is greatly superior to any yet introduced into this country. Here, statistics are neglected; and when any emergency demands a special inquiry, information is obtained by means of committees of the Commons, whose labours are so multifarious, as to afford them time for little else than the investigation of general conclusions, derived from the experience of those supposed to be most conversant with the subject. An approximation to truth may thus be made, but the results are never so minutely accurate as those obtained from statistical investigations; and, as they are generally deduced from a comparison of opposing testimonies, and sometimes from partial evidence, they frequently utterly fail in one most important respect, namely—in convincing the public of the facts which they proclaim.

The introduction into this country of a singularly malignant contagious malady, which, though it selects its victims from every order of society, is chiefly propagated amongst those whose health is depressed by disease, mental anxiety, or want of the comforts and conveniences of life, has directed public attention to an investigation of the state of the poor. In Manchester, Boards of Health were established, in each of the fourteen districts of Police, for the purpose of minutely inspecting the state of the houses and streets. These districts were divided into minute sections, to each of which two or more inspectors were appointed from among the most respectable inhabitants of the vicinity, and they were provided with tabular queries, applying to each particular house and street. Individual exceptions only exist, in which minute returns were not furnished to the Special Board: and as the investigation was prompted equally by the demands of benevolence, of personal security, and of the general welfare, the results may be esteemed as accurate as the nature of the investigation would permit. The other facts contained in this pamphlet have been obtained from the public offices of the town, or are the results of the author's personal observation.

The township of Manchester chiefly consists of dense masses of houses, inhabited by the population engaged in the great manufactories of the cotton trade. Some of the central divisions are occupied by warehouses and shops, and a few streets by the dwellings of some of the more wealthy inhabitants; but the opulent merchants chiefly reside in the country, and even the superior servants of their establishments inhabit the suburban townships. Manchester, properly so called, is chiefly inhabited by shopkeepers and the labouring classes.* Those districts where the poor dwell are of very recent origin. The rapid growth of the cotton manufacture has attracted hither

* To the stranger, it is also necessary to observe, that the investigations on whose results the conclusions of this pamphlet are founded, were of necessity conducted *in the township of Manchester only;* and that the inhabitants of a great part of the adjacent townships are in a condition superior to that described in these pages. The most respectable portion of the operative population has, we think, a tendency to avoid the central districts of Manchester, and to congregate in the suburban townships.

operatives from every part of the kingdom, and Ireland has poured forth the most destitute of her hordes to supply the constantly increasing demand for labour. This immigration has been, in one important respect, a serious evil. The Irish have taught the labouring classes of this country a pernicious lesson. The system of cottier farming, the demoralization and barbarism of the people, and the general use of the potato as the chief article of food, have encouraged the population in Ireland more rapidly than the *available* means of subsistence have been increased. Debased alike by ignorance and pauperism, they have discovered, with the savage, what is the minimum of the means of life, upon which existence may be prolonged. The paucity of the amount of means and comforts *necessary for the mere support of life,* is not known by a more civilized population, and this secret has been taught the labourers of this country by the Irish. As competition and the restrictions and burdens of trade diminished the profits of capital, and consequently reduced the price of labour, the contagious example of ignorance and a barbarous disregard of forethought and economy, exhibited by the Irish, spread. The colonization of savage tribes has ever been attended with effects on civilization as fatal as those which have marked the progress of the sand flood over the fertile plains of Egypt. Instructed in the fatal secret of subsisting on what is barely necessary to life—yielding partly to necessity, and partly to example,—the labouring classes have ceased to entertain a laudable pride in furnishing their houses, and in multiplying the decent comforts which minister to happiness. What is superfluous to the mere exigencies of nature, is too often expended at the tavern; and for the provision of old age and infirmity, they too frequently trust either to charity, to the support of their children, or to the protection of the poor laws.

When this example is considered in connexion with the unremitted labour of the whole population engaged in the various branches of the cotton manufacture, our wonder will be less excited by their fatal demoralization. Prolonged and exhausting labour, continued from day to day, and from year to year, is not calculated to develop the intellectual or moral faculties of man. The dull routine of a ceaseless drudgery, in which the same mechanical process is incessantly repeated, resembles the torment of Sisyphus —the toil, like the rock, recoils perpetually on the wearied operative. The mind gathers neither stores nor strength from the constant extension and retraction of the same muscles. The intellect slumbers in supine inertness; but the grosser parts of our nature attain a rank development. To condemn man to such severity of toil is, in some measure, to cultivate in him the habits of an animal. He becomes reckless. He disregards the distinguishing appetites and habits of his species. He neglects the comforts and delicacies of life. He lives in squalid wretchedness, on meager food, and expends his superfluous gains in debauchery.

The population employed in the cotton factories rises at five o'clock in the morning, works in the mills from six till eight o'clock, and returns home for half an hour or forty minutes to breakfast. This meal generally consists of tea or coffee, with a little bread. Oatmeal porridge is sometimes, but of late rarely used, and chiefly by the men; but the stimulus of tea is preferred, and especially by the women. The tea is almost always of a bad, and sometimes of a deleterious quality; the infusion is weak, and little or no milk is added. The operatives return to the mills and workshops until twelve o'clock, when an hour is allowed for dinner. Amongst those who obtain the lower rates of wages this meal generally consists of boiled potatoes. The mess of potatoes is put into one large dish; melted lard and butter are poured upon them, and a few pieces of fried fat bacon are sometimes mingled with them, and but seldom a little meat. Those who obtain better wages, or families whose aggregate income is larger, add a greater proportion of animal food to this meal, at least three times in the week; but the quantity consumed by the labouring population is not great. The family sits round the table, and each rapidly appropriates his portion on a plate, or they all plunge their spoons into the dish, and with an animal eagerness satisfy the cravings of their appetite. At the expiration of the hour, they are all again employed in the workshops or mills, where they continue until seven o'clock or a later hour, when they generally again indulge in the use of tea, often mingled with spirits accompanied by a little bread. Oatmeal or potatoes are however taken by some a second time in the evening.

The comparatively innutritious qualities of these articles of diet are most evident. We are, however, by no means prepared to say that an individual living in a healthy atmosphere, and engaged in active employment in the open air, would not be able to continue protracted and severe labour, without any suffering, whilst nourished by this food. We should rather be disposed on the contrary to affirm, that any ill effects must necessarily be so much diminished, that, from the influence of habit, and the benefits derived from the constant inhalation of an uncontaminated atmosphere, during healthy exercise in agricultural pursuits, few if any evil results would ensue. But the population nourished on this aliment is crowded into one dense mass, in cottages separated by narrow, unpaved, and almost pestilential streets, in an atmosphere loaded with the smoke and exhalations of a large manufacturing city. The operatives are congregated in rooms and workshops during twelve hours in the day, in an enervating, heated atmosphere, which is frequently loaded with dust or filaments of cotton, or impure from constant respiration, or from other causes. They are engaged in an employment which absorbs their attention, and unremittingly employs their physical energies.* They are drudges

* A gentleman, whose opinions on these subjects command universal respect, suggests to me, that the intensity of this application is exceedingly increased by the system of paying, not for time, but according to the result of labour.

who watch the movements, and assist the operations, of a mighty material force, which toils with an energy ever unconscious of fatigue. The persevering labour of the operative must rival the mathematical precision, the incessant motion, and the exhaustless power of the machine.

Hence, besides the negative results—the abstraction of moral and intellectual stimuli—the absence of variety—banishment from the grateful air and the cheering influences of light, the physical energies are impaired by toil, and imperfect nutrition. The artisan too seldom possessess sufficient moral dignity or intellectual or organic strength to resist the seductions of appetite. His wife and children, subjected to the same process, have little power to cheer his remaining moments of leisure· Domestic economy is neglected, domestic comforts are too frequently unknown. A meal of coarse food is hastily prepared, and devoured with precipitation. Home has little other relation to him than that of shelter—few pleasures are there—it chiefly presents to him a scene of physical exhaustion, from which he is glad to escape. His house is ill furnished, uncleanly, often ill ventilated—perhaps damp ; his food, from want of forethought and domestic economy, is meagre and innutritious ; he generally becomes debilitated and hypochondriacal, and unless supported by principle, falls the victim of dissipation. In all these respects, it is grateful to add, that those among the operatives of the mills, who are employed *in the process of spinning*, and especially of fine spinning, (who receive a high rate of wages and who are elevated on account of their skill) are more attentive to their domestic arrangements, have better furnished houses, are consequently more regular in their habits, and more observant of their duties than those engaged in other branches of the manufacture.

The other classes of artisans of whom we have spoken, are frequently subject to a disease, in which the sensibility of the stomach and bowels is morbidly excited ; the alvine secretions are deranged, and the appetite impaired. Whilst this state continues, the patient loses flesh, his features are sharpened, the skin becomes sallow, or of the yellow hue which is observed in those who have suffered from the influence of tropical climates. The strength fails, the capacities of physical enjoyment are destroyed, and the paroxysms of corporeal suffering are aggravated by deep mental depression. We cannot wonder that the wretched victim of this disease, invited by those haunts of misery and crime the gin shop and the tavern, as he passes to his daily labour, should endeavour to cheat his suffering of a few moments, by the false excitement procured by ardent spirits ; or that the exhausted artisan, driven by ennui and discomfort from his squalid home, should strive, in the delirious dreams of a continued debauch, to forget the remembrance of his reckless improvidence, of the destitution, hunger, and uninterrupted toil, which threaten to destroy the remaining energies of his enfeebled constitution.

The contagious example which the Irish have exhibited of barbarous habits and savage want of economy, united with the necessarily debasing consequences of uninterrupted toil, have demoralized the people.

The inspection conducted by the District Boards of Health, chiefly referred to the state of the streets and houses, inhabited by the labouring population—to local nuisances, and more general evils. The greatest portion of these districts, especially of those situated beyond Great Ancoats-street, are of very recent origin; and from the want of proper police regulations are untraversed by common sewers. The houses are ill soughed, often ill ventilated, unprovided with privies, and, in consequence, the streets which are narrow, unpaved, and worn into deep ruts, become the common receptacles of mud, refuse, and disgusting ordure.

The Inspectors' reports do not comprise all the houses and streets of the respective districts, and are in some other respects imperfect. The returns concerning the various defects which they enumerate must be received, as the reports of evils, too positive to be overlooked. Frequently, when they existed in a slighter degree, the questions received no reply.

Predisposition to contagious disease is encouraged by every thing which depresses the physical energies, amongst the principal of which agencies may be enumerated imperfect nutrition; exposure to cold and moisture, whether from inadequate shelter, or from want of clothing and fuel, or from dampness of the habitation ; uncleanliness of the person, the street, and the abode ; an atmosphere contaminated, whether from the want of ventilation, or from impure effluvia ; extreme labour, and consequent physical exhaustion ; intemperance ; fear ; anxiety ; diarrhœa, and other diseases. The whole of these subjects could not be included in the investigation, though it originated in a desire to remove, as far as possible, those ills which depressed the health of the population. The list of inquiries to which the inspectors were requested to make tabular replies is placed in the appendix, for the purpose of enabling the reader to form his own opinion of the investigation from which the classified results are deduced.

The state of the streets powerfully affects the health of their inhabitants. Sporadic cases of typhus chiefly appear in those which are narrow, ill ventilated, unpaved, or which contain heaps of refuse, or stagnant pools. The confined air and noxious exhalations, which abound in such places, depress the health of the people, and on this account contagious diseases are also most rapidly propagated there. The operation of these causes is exceedingly promoted by their reflex influence on the manners. The houses, in such situations, are uncleanly, ill provided with furniture ; an air of discomfort if not of squalid and loathsome wretchedness pervades them, they are often dilapidated, badly drained, damp : and the habits of their tenants are gross—they are ill-fed, ill-clothed, and uneconomical—at once spendthrifts and destitute —denying themselves the comforts of life, in order that they may wallow in the unrestrained licence of animal appetite. An intimate connexion subsists, among the poor, between the cleanliness of the street and that of the house and person. Uneconomical habits, and dissipation are almost inseparably allied; and they are so frequently connected with uncleanliness, that we cannot consider their concomitance as altogether accidental. The first step to recklessness may often be traced in a neglect of that self-respect, and of the love of domestic enjoyments, which are indicated by personal slovenliness, and discomfort of the habitation Hence, the importance of providing by police regulations or general enactment, against those fertile sources alike of disease and demoralization, presented by the gross neglect of the streets and habitations of the poor. When the health is depressed by the concurrence of these causes, contagious diseases spread with a fatal malignancy among the population subjected to their influence. The records* of the Fever Hospital of Manchester, prove that typhus *prevails almost exclusively* in such situations.

The following table, arranged by the Committee of classification appointed by the Special Board of Health, from the reports of Inspectors of the various District Boards of Manchester, shows the extent to which the imperfect state of the streets of Manches-

* Abundant evidence of this fact was collected by Mr. Wallis, lately House Surgeon to the House of Recovery.

ter may tend to promote demoralization and disease among the poor.

No. of District	No. of streets inspected.	No. of streets unpaved.	No. of streets partially pvd.	No. of streets ill ventilated.	No. of streets containing heaps of refuse, stagnant pools, ordure, &c.
1	114	63	13	7	64
2	180	93	7	23	92
3	49	2	2	12	28
4	66	37	10	12	52
5	30	2	5	5	12
6	2	1	0	1	2
7	53	13	5	12	17
8	16	2	1	2	7
9	48	0	0	9	20
10	29	19	0	10	23
11	0	0	0	0	0
12	12	0	1	1	4
13	55	3	9	10	23
14	33	13	0	8	8
Total ..	687	248	53	112	352

A minute inspection of this table will render the extent of the evil affecting the poor more apparent. Those districts which are almost exclusively inhabited by the labouring population are Nos. **1**, **2**, **3**, **4**, and **10**. Nos. **13** and **14**, and **7**, also contain, besides the dwellings of the operatives, those of shopkeepers and tradesmen, and are traversed by many of the principal thoroughfares. No. **11** was not inspected, and Nos. **5**, **6**, **8**, and **9**, are the central districts containing the chief streets, the most respectable shops, the dwellings of the more wealthy inhabitants, and the warehouses of merchants and manufacturers. Subtracting, therefore, from the various totals, those items in the reports which concern these divisions only, we discover in those districts which contain a large portion of poor, namely, in Nos. **1**, **2**, **3**, **4**, **7**,

10, 13, and 14, that among 579 streets inspected, 243 were altogether unpaved—46 partially paved—93 ill ventilated—and 307 contained heaps of refuse, deep ruts, stagnant pools, ordure, &c.; and in the districts which are almost exclusively inhabited by the poor, namely, Nos. 1, 2, 3, 4, and 10, among 438 streets inspected, 214 were altogether unpaved—32 partially paved—63 ill ventilated—and 259 contained heaps of refuse, deep ruts, stagnant pools, ordure, &c.

The replies to the questions proposed in the second table relating to houses, contain equally remarkable results, which have been carefully arranged by the Classification Committee of the Special Board of Health, as follows.

District	No. of houses inspected.	No. of houses reported as requiring whitewashing	No. of houses reported as requiring repair.	No. of houses in which the soughs wanted repair.	No. of houses damp.	No. of houses reported as ill ventilated.	No. of houses wanting privies.
1	850	399	128	112	177	70	326
2	2489	898	282	145	497	109	755
3	213	145	104	41	61	52	96
4	650	279	106	105	134	69	250
5	413	176	82	70	101	11	66
6	12	3	5	5			5
7	343	76	59	57	86	21	79
8	132	35	30	39	48	22	20
9	128	34	32	24	39	19	25
10	370	195	53	123	54	2	232
11							
12	113	33	23	27	24	16	52
13	757	218	44	108	146	54	177
14	481	74	13	83	68	7	138
Total..	6951	2565	960	939	1435	452	2221

It is however to be lamented, that even these numerical results fail to exhibit a perfect picture of the ills which are suffered by the poor. The replies to the questions contained in the inspectors' table refer only to cases of the most positive kind, and the numerical results would therefore have been exceedingly increased, had they embraced those in which the evils existed in a scarcely inferior degree. Some idea of the want of cleanliness prevalent in their habitations, may be obtained from the report of the number of houses requiring whitewashing; but this column fails to indicate their gross neglect of order, and absolute filth. Much less can we obtain satisfactory statistical results concerning the want of furniture, especially of bedding, and of food, clothing, and fuel. In these respects the habitations of the Irish are most destitute. They can scarcely be said to be furnished. They contain one or two chairs, a mean table, the most scanty culinary apparatus, and one or two beds, loathsome with filth. A whole family is often accomodated on a single bed, and sometimes a heap of filthy straw and a covering of old sacking hide them in one undistinguished heap, debased alike by penury, want of economy, and dissolute habits. Frequently, the inspectors found two or more families crowded into one small house, containing only two apartments, one in which they slept, and another in which they eat; and often more than one family lived in a damp cellar, containing only one room, in whose pestilential atmosphere from twelve to sixteen persons were crowded. To these fertile sources of disease were sometimes added the keeping of pigs and other animals in the house, with other nuisances of the most revolting character.

As the visits of the inspectors were made in the day, when the population is engaged in the mills, and the vagrants and paupers are wandering through the town, they could not form any just idea of the state of the pauper lodging houses. The establishments thus designated are fertile sources of disease and demoralization. They are frequently able to accommodate from twenty to thirty or more lodgers, among whom are the most abandoned characters, who, reckless of the morrow, resort thither for the shelter of the night—men who find safety in a constant change of abode, or are too uncertain in their pursuits to remain beneath the same roof for a longer period. Here, without distinction of age or sex, careless of all decency, they are crowded in small and wretched apartments; the same bed receiving a succession of tenants until too offensive even for their unfastidious senses. The Special Board being desirous that these lodging houses should be inspected by the Overseers, the Churchwardens obtained a report of the number in each district, which cannot fail to be a source of surprise and apprehension.

PAUPER LODGING HOUSES.

	No. of houses.		*No. of houses.*
District No. 1	0	District No. 9	0
2	108	10	12
3	51	11	26
4	0	12	—
5	6	13	60
6	0	14	1
7	3		
8	0		267

The temporary tenants of these disgusting abodes,

too frequently debased by vice, haunted by want, and every other consequence of crime, are peculiarly disposed to the reception of contagion. Their asylums are frequently recesses where it lurks, and they are active agents in its diffusion. They ought to be as much the objects of a careful vigilance from those who are the guardians of the health, as from those who protect the property of the public.

In some districts of the town exist evils so remarkable as to require more minute description. A portion of low, swampy ground, liable to be frequently inundated, and to constant exhalation, is included between a high bank over which the Oxford Road passes, and a bend of the river Medlock, where its course is impeded by a weir. This unhealthy spot lies so low that the chimneys of its houses, some of them three stories high, are little above the level of the road. About two hundred of these habitations are crowded together in an extremely narrow space, and they are chiefly inhabited by the lowest Irish. Many of these houses have also cellars, whose floor is scarcely elevated above the level of the water flowing in the Medlock. The soughs are destroyed, or out of repair: and these narrow abodes are in consequence always damp, and are frequently flooded to the depth of several inches, because the surface water can find no exit. This district has sometimes been the haunt of hordes of thieves and desperadoes who defied the law, and is always inhabited by a class resembling savages in their appetites and habits. It is surrounded on every side by some of the largest factories of the town, whose chimneys vomit forth dense clouds of smoke, which hang heavily over this insalubrious region.

The subjoined document resulted from an inspection made by a Special Sub-committee of Members of the Board of Health, and the signatures of the gentlemen forming that Sub-committee were appended to it.*

---

* TO THE MAGISTRATES OF THE DISTRICT.

GENTLEMEN,

The undersigned having been deputed by the Special Board of Health to inquire into the state of Little Ireland, beg to report that in the main street and courts abutting, the sewers are all in a most wretched state, and quite inadequate to carry off the surface water, not to mention the slops thrown down by the inhabitants in about two hundred houses.

The privies are in a most disgraceful state, inaccessible from filth, and too few for the accommodation of the number of people. —the average number being two to two hundred and fifty people, The upper rooms are, with few exceptions, very dirty, and the cellars much worse; all damp, and some occasionally overflowed. The cellars consist of two rooms on a floor, each nine to ten feet square, some inhabited by ten persons, others by more: in many, the people have no beds, and keep each other warm by close stowage on shavings, straw, &c.; a change of linen or clothes is an exception to the common practice. Many of the back rooms where they sleep have no other means of ventilation than from the front rooms.

Some of the cellars on the lower ground were once filled up as uninhabitable; but one is now occupied by a weaver, and he has stopped up the drain with clay, to prevent the water flowing

Near the centre of the town, a mass of buildings inhabited by prostitutes and thieves, is intersected by narrow and loathsome streets, and close courts defiled with refuse. These nuisances exist in No. 13 District, on the western side of Deansgate, and chiefly abound in Wood-street, Spinning Field, Cumberland-street, Parliament Passage, Parliament-street, and Thomson-street. In Parliament-street there is only one privy for three hundred and eighty inhabitants, which is placed in a narrow passage, whence its effluvia infest the adjacent houses, and must prove a most fertile source of disease. In this street also, cess pools with open grids have been made close to the doors of the houses, in which dis-

---

from it into his cellar, and mops up the water every morning.

We conceive it will be impossible effectually to remove the evils enumerated; and offer the following suggestions with a view to their partial amelioration.

First, to open up the main sewer from the bottom, and to relay it.

Secondly, to open and unchoke the lateral drains, and secure a regular discharge of the water, &c., into the main sewer.

Thirdly, to enforce the weekly cleansing and purification of the privies.

Fourthly, if practicable, to fill up the cellars.

Fifthly, to provide the inhabitants with quicklime, and induce them to whitewash their rooms, where it can be done with safety.

Sixthly, if possible, to induce the inhabitants to observe greater cleanliness in their houses and persons.

In conclusion, we are decidedly of opinion that should Cholera visit this neighbourhood, a more suitable soil and situation for its malignant development cannot be found than that described and commonly known by the name of Little Ireland.

gusting refuse accumulates, and whence its noxious effluvia constantly exhale. In Parliament Passage about thirty houses have been erected, merely separated by an extremely narrow passage (a yard and a half wide) from the wall and back door of other houses. These thirty houses have one privy.

The state of the streets and houses in that part of No. 4, included between Store-street and Travis-street, and London Road, is exceedingly wretched—especially those built on some irregular and broken mounds of clay, on a steep declivity descending into Store-street. These narrow avenues are rough, irregular gullies, down which filthy streams percolate; and the inhabitants are crowded in dilapidated abodes, or obscure and damp cellars, in which it is impossible for the health to be preserved.

Unwilling to weary the patience of the reader by extending such disgusting details, it may suffice to refer generally to the wretched state of the habitations of the poor in Clay-street, and the lower portion of Pot-street; in Providence-street, and its adjoining courts; in Back Portugal-street; in Back Hart-street, and many of the courts in the neighbourhood of Portland-street, some of which are not more than a yard and a quarter wide, and contain houses, frequently three stories high, the lowest of which stories is occasionally used as a receptacle of *excrementitious matter*:—to many streets in the neighbourhood of Garden-street, Shudehill:—to Back Irk-street, and to the state of almost the whole of that mass of cottages filling the insalubrious valley through which the Irk flows, and which is denominated Irish town.

The Irk, black with the refuse of Dye-works erected on its banks, receives excrementitious matters from some sewers in this portion of the town—the drainage from the gas-works, and filth of the most pernicious character from bone-works, tanneries, size manufactories, &c. Immediately beneath Ducie-Bridge, in a deep hollow between two high banks, it sweeps round a large cluster of some of the most wretched and dilapidated buildings of the town. The course of the river is here impeded by a weir, and a large tannery eight stories high (three of which stories are filled with skins exposed to the atmosphere, in some stage of the processes to which they are subjected) towers close to this crazy labyrinth of pauper dwellings. This group of habitations is called "Gibraltar," and no site can well be more insalubrious than that on which it is built. Pursuing the course of the river on the other side of Ducie-bridge, other tanneries, size manufactories, and tripe-houses occur. The parish burial ground occupies one side of the stream, and a series of courts of the most singular and unhealthy character, the other. Access is obtained to these courts through narrow covered entries from Long Millgate, whence the explorer descends by stone stairs, and in one instance by three successive flights of steps to a level with the bed of the river. In this last mentioned (Allen's) court he discovers himself to be surrounded, on one side by a wall of rock, on two others by houses three stories high, and on the fourth by the abrupt and high bank down which he descended, and by walls and houses erected on the summit. These houses were, a short time ago, chiefly inhabited by fringe, silk, and cotton weavers, and winders, and each house contained in general three or four families. An adjoining court (Barrett's,) on the summit of the bank, separated from Allen's court only by a low wall, contained, besides a pig-stye —a tripe manufactory in a low cottage, which was in a state of loathsome filth. Portions of animal matter were decaying in it, and one of the inner rooms was converted into a kennel, and contained a litter of puppies. In the court, on the opposite side, is a tan yard where skins are prepared without bark in open pits, and here is also a catgut manufactory. Many of the windows of the houses in Allen's court, open over the river Irk, whose stream (again impeded, at the distance of one hundred yards by a weir) separates it from another tannery, four stories high and filled with skins, exposed to the currents of air which pass through the building. On the other side of this tannery is the parish burial ground, chiefly used as a place of interment for paupers. A more unhealthy spot than this (Allen's) court it would be difficult to discover, and the physical depression consequent on living in such a situation, may be inferred from what ensued on the introduction of cholera here. A match-seller, living in the first story of one of these houses, was seized with cholera, on Sunday, July 22nd: he died on Wednesday, July 25th; and owing to the wilful negligence of his friends, and because the Board of Health had no intimation of the occurrence, he was not buried until Friday afternoon, July 27th. On that day, five other cases of cholera occurred amongst the inhabitants of the court. On the 28th, seven, and on the 29th two. The cases were nearly all fatal. Those affected with cholera were on the 28th and 29th removed to the Hospital, the dead were buried, and on the 29th the majority of the inhabitants were taken to a house of reception, and the rest with one exception dispersed into the town, until their houses had been thoroughly fumigated, ventilated, whitewashed, and cleansed; notwithstanding which dispersion, other cases occurred amongst those who had left the court.

These facts are thus minutely related, because we are anxious to direct public attention to the advantage which would accrue, from widening this portion of Long Millgate, by taking down the whole of the houses on the Irk side of the street, from a factory which projects into it, on that side, as far as Ducie Bridge, and thus improving this important entrance to the town, from Bury, and from the North East of Lancashire.

The houses of the poor, especially throughout the whole of the Districts Nos. 1, 2, 3, 4, are too generally built back to back, having therefore only one outlet, no yard, no privy, and no receptacle of refuse.

Consequently the narrow, unpaved streets, in which mud and water stagnate, become the common receptacles of offal and ordure. Often low, damp, ill ventilated cellars exist beneath the houses; an improvement on which system consists in the erection of a stage over the first story, by which access is obtained to the second, and the house is inhabited by two separate families. More than one disgraceful example of this might be enumerated. The streets, in the districts where the poor reside, are generally unsewered, and the drainage is consequently superficial. The houses are often built with a total neglect of order, on the summit of natural irregularities of the surface, or on mounds left at the side of artificial excavations on the brick grounds, with which these parts of the town abound.

One nuisance frequently occurs in these districts of so noxious a character, that it ought, at the earliest period, to be suppressed by legal interference. The houses of the poor sometimes surround a common area, into which the doors and windows open at the back of the dwelling. Porkers, who feed pigs in the town, often contract with the inhabitants to pay some small sum for the rent of their area, which is immediately covered with pigstyes, and converted into a dung-heap and receptacle of the putrescent garbage, upon which the animals are fed, as also of the refuse which is now heedlessly flung into it from all the surrounding dwellings. The offensive odour which sometimes arises from these areas cannot be conceived.

There is no *Common* Slaughter-house in Manchester, and those which exist are chiefly situated in the narrowest and most filthy streets in the town. The drainage from these houses, deeply tinged with blood, and impregnated with other animal matters, frequently flows down the common surface drain of the street, and stagnates in the ruts and pools. Moreover, sometimes in the yards of these houses—from the want of a vigilant circumspection—offal is allowed to accumulate with the grossest neglect of decency and disregard to the health of the surrounding inhabitants. The attention of the commissioners of police cannot be too soon directed to the propriety of obtaining powers to erect a Common Slaughter-house on some vacant space, and to compel the butchers of the town to slaughter all animals killed in the township in the building thus provided.

The districts, Nos. 1, 2, 3, and 4, are inhabited by a turbulent population, which, rendered reckless by dissipation and want,—misled by the secret intrigues, and excited by the inflammatory harangues of demagogues, has frequently committed daring assaults on the liberty of the more peaceful portions of the working classes, and the most frightful devastations on the property of their masters. Machines have been broken, and factories gutted and burned at mid-day, and the riotous crowd has dispersed ere the insufficient body of police arrived at the scene of disturbance. The civic force of the town is totally inadequate to maintain the peace, and to defend property from the attacks of lawless depredators; and *a more efficient, and more numerous corps ought to be immediately organized,* to give power to the law, so often mocked by the daring front of sedition, and outraged by the frantic violence of an ignorant and deluded rabble. The police form, in fact, so weak a screen against the power of the mob, that popular violence is now, in almost every instance, controlled by the presence of a military force.

The wages* obtained by operatives in the various branches of the cotton manufacture are, in general, such, as with the exercise of that economy without which wealth itself is wasted, would be sufficient to provide them with all the decent comforts of life—the average wages of all persons employed in the mills (young and old) being from nine to twelve shillings per week. Their means are too often consumed by vice and *improvidence.* But the wages of certain classes are exceedingly meagre. The introduction of the power-loom, though ultimately destined to be productive of the greatest general bene-

---

* "The wages are paid weekly, not once a fortnight, or once a month, as is the case in collieries and many other places. The youngest child in the mill earns three shillings per week, and the best female spinner twenty one shillings. The total paid is £356.—averaging nine shillings and three pence per week to each person employed." *Letter to Lord Althorp in Defence of the Cotton Factories of Lancashire.* By HOLLAND HOOLE, ESQ.

fits, has, in the present restricted state of commerce, occasioned some temporary embarrassment, by diminishing the demand for certain kinds of labour, and, consequently, their price. The hand-loom weavers, *existing in this state of transition,* still continue a very extensive class, and though they labour fourteen hours and upwards daily, earn only from five to seven or eight shillings per week.* They consist chiefly of Irish, and are affected by all the causes of moral and physical depression which we have enumerated. Ill-fed—ill-clothed—half-sheltered and ignorant;—weaving in close damp cellars, or crowded workshops, it only remains that they should become, as is too frequently the case, demoralized and reckless, to render perfect the portraiture of savage life. Amongst men so situated, the moral check has no influence in preventing the rapid increase of the population. The existence of cheap and redundant labour in the market has, also, a *constant* tendency to lessen its general price, and hence the wages of the English operatives have been exceedingly reduced by this immigration of Irish—their comforts consequently diminished—their manners debased—and the natural influence of manufactures on the people thwarted. We are well convinced that without the numerical and moral influence of this class, on the means and on the character of the people who have had to enter into competition with them in the market of labour,

* Evidence of Joseph Foster before the Emigration Committee, 1827.

we should have had less occasion to regret the physical and moral degradation of the operative population.

The poor-laws, as at present administered, retain all the evils of the gross and indiscriminate bounty of ancient monasteries. They also fail in exciting the gratitude of the people, and they extinguish the charity of the rich. The custom is not now demanded as the prop of any superstition ; nor is it fit that institutions, well calculated to assuage the miseries which feudalism inflicted on its unemployed and unhappy serfs, should be allowed to perpetuate indigence, improvidence, idleness and vice, in a commercial community. The artificial structure of society, in providing security against existing evils, has too frequently neglected the remote moral influence of its arrangements on the community. Humanity rejoices in the consciousness that the poorest may obtain the advantages of skilful care in disease, and that there are asylums for infirmity, age, and decrepitude ; but the unlimited extension of benefits, devised by a wise intelligence for the relief of evils which no human prescience could elude, has a direct tendency to encourage amongst the poor apathy concerning present exigencies, and the neglect of a provision for the contingencies of the future.

A rate levied on property for the support of indigence is, in a great degree, a tax on the capital, from whose employment are derived the incentives of industry and the rewards of the frugal, ingenious, and virtuous poor. If the only test of the application of this fund be *indigence,* without reference to *desert* —be *want,* irrespective of *character*—motives to frugality, self controul and industry are at once removed, and the strong barrier which nature had itself erected to prevent the moral lapse of the entire population is wantonly destroyed. The tax acts as a new burden on the *industrious* poor, already suffering from an enormous pressure, and not only drags within the limits of pauperism unwilling victims, but paralyses with despair the efforts of those whose exertions might otherwise have prolonged their struggle with adversity. The wages of the worthy are often given to encourage the sluggard, the drunkard, and the man whose imprudence entails on the community the precocious burden of his meagre and neglected offspring.

The feeble obstacle raised in the *country* to the propagation of a pauper population, by making the indigent chargeable on the estates of the land owners, is even there rendered almost entirely inefficacious by the too frequent non-residence of the gentry, or the indifference with which this apparently inevitable evil is regarded. In the South of England the fatal error has been committed of paying a certain portion of the wages of able bodied labourers out of the fund obtained by the poor-rates; and a population is thus created, bound like slaves to toil, and having also like them a right to be maintained. But, in the large towns, the feeble check to the increase of pauperism, which thus exists in some rural districts, is entirely removed. The land is let to speculators who build cottages, the rents of which are collected weekly, a commutation for the rates being often paid by the landlord when they are demanded, which seldom occurs in the lowest description of houses. A married man having thus by law an unquestioned right to a maintenance proportioned to the number of his family, direct encouragement is afforded to improvident marriages. The most destitute and immoral marry to increase their claim on the stipend appointed for them by law, which thus acts as a bounty on the increase of a squalid and debilitated race, who inherit from their parents disease, sometimes deformity, often vice, and always beggary.

The number of labourers thus created diminishes the already scanty wages of that portion of the population still content to endeavour by precarious toil to maintain their honest independence. Desperate is the struggle by which, under such a system, the upright labourer procures for his family the comforts of existence. Many are dragged by the accidents of life to an unwilling acceptance of this legalized pension of the profligate, and some, over informed by misfortune in the treachery of their own hearts, are seduced to palter with temptation, and at length to capitulate with their apparent fate.

Fearful demoralization attends an impost whose distribution diminishes the incentives to prudence and virtue. When reckless of the future, the intelligence of man is confined to the narrow limits of the present. He thus debases himself beneath the animals whose instincts teach them to lay up stores for the season of need. The gains* of the pauper are, in prosperity, frequently squandered in taverns, whilst his family exists in hungered and ragged misery, and few sympathies with the sufferings of his aged relatives or neighbours enter his cold heart, since he knows they have an equal claim with himself, on that pittance which the law awards. The superfluities which nature would prompt him in a season of abundance to hoard for the accidents of the future, are wasted with reckless profusion; because *the law takes care of the future.* Selfish profligacy usurps the seat of the household virtues of the English labourer.

Charity once extended an invisible chain of sympathy between the higher and lower ranks of society, which has been destroyed by the luckless pseudo-philanthropy of the law. Few aged or decrepid pensioners now gratefully receive the visits of the higher classes—few of the poor seek the counsel, the admonitions, and assistance of the rich in the period of the inevitable accidents of life. The bar of the overseer is however crowded with the sturdy applicants for a legalized relief, who regard the distributor of this bounty as their stern and merciless oppressor, instructed by the compassionless rich to

* See evidence of Mr. Allen concerning pauperism in Spitalfields.

reduce to the lowest possible amount the alms which the law wrings from their reluctant hands. This disruption of the natural ties has created a wide gulph between the higher and lower orders of the community, across which, the scowl of hatred banishes the smile of charity and love.

That government have appointed a Commission of inquiry into the evils arising from the administration of the Poor-laws, must be a source of satisfaction to every well wisher to the poor. Since it would be unjust to annul the existing provision for a rapidly increasing indigence which the law has itself fostered, the improvement of its present administration is all that the most sanguine can expect as an immediate result of this inquiry. Every change which assimilates the *method of distributing* this legal charity to that by which a well regulated private bounty is administered, must be hailed. The present official organization in the large towns is incapable of producing these results. The parish officers and sidesmen are not sufficiently numerous to enable them (if they were permitted by law) to make a discrimination—concerning the characters of individuals, their actual condition, and the accidents or faults that may have occasioned it—equal to that which is observed in the most judicious distribution of private bounty. Since desert does not enhance the claim which indigence can enforce, the only relation which the parish officer now has with the applicant for relief is that of the investigation and proof of his indigence ; and, to this end, those now employed may be sufficiently proper agents. But if we would substitute any portion of that sympathy with the distresses of the poor, and that gratitude for relief afforded—that acknowledged right to administer good counsel, and that willingness to receive advice—that privilege of inquiring into the arrangements of domestic economy, instructing the ignorant, and checking the perverse—all which attend the beneficent path of private charity, much superior men must be employed in the office of visiting the houses of the poor, and being the almoners of the public. Such an office can only be properly filled by men of some education, but especially of high moral character, and possessing great natural gentleness. An attempt should be constantly made to relieve the mind of the independent poor from the necessity of receiving an eleemosynary dole, by recommending the worthy to employment. It is not sufficient that the sidesman or churchwarden should give a few hours daily to an examination of all applicants in our enormous townships, but the towns should be minutely subdivided, each district having its local board, which (besides an executive parish overseer resident in the district, and thus possessing every means of becoming minutely acquainted with the character of the inhabitants,) should also be furnished with its board of superior officers. By such means: by adopting the test of desert, at least to determine the *amount* of relief bestowed: by discouraging or even rejecting those whose indigence is the consequence of dissipation, of idleness, and of wilful imprudence; and by making the overseers themselves the means of instructing the poor, that every labourer is the surest architect of his own fortune —by constituting them the patrons of virtue and the censors of vice, and besides being the almoners of the public charity, the sources of a powerful moral agency—much good might be effected. The enormous expenditure, incurred by the present system, might be exceedingly reduced, and the alms might at length (by a process whose success would depend on the gradual moral improvement of society,) be confined to such of the aged, the decrepid, and the unfortunate, as being without the hope of assistance from the charity of relations or friends, were thus reluctantly driven, by a hard necessity, to have recourse to the *fund of the poor. Societies for mutual relief should be everywhere encouraged,* and a constant effort should be vigorously maintained to disburden the public of this enormous tax, by every other *means which would contribute to the virtuous independence of the working classes.*

At present this alarming impost increases so rapidly, that it threatens ultimately to absorb the fund which ought to be employed solely in rewarding the labour of the industrious poor, and hence, to reduce the whole population to the condition of helots.

The fund derived from the poor's-rate for the relief of the indigent, is, in Manchester, as judiciously administered as the state of the law will permit. Too much praise can scarcely be given to the zealous exertions of those gentlemen who fill the offices of churchwardens and sidesmen. Yet, the effect of the present state of the law is but too apparent here.

Pauperism is every where accompanied with moral and physical degradation. Impressed with this opinion, we endeavoured to discover, from such facts as might be ascertained at the town's offices, how this calamitous law affected Manchester.

Unfortunately, the distribution of the poor rates is not registered separately for each of the police divisions. We are therefore only able to compare the four sections of the town visited by the overseers. The first and second of these four sections, which we shall denominate the Newtown and the Ancoats districts, comprise Nos. 1, 2, and 4, and therefore contain almost exclusively poor inhabitants. On the other hand, the third, or central division, besides Nos. 5, 6, 9, and a small part of No. 8, which are inhabited by a great number of shopkeepers and tradesmen, contains also Nos. 10, 11, and 14, which have a very large proportion of poor. The fourth, or Portland-street District, besides Nos. 3, 7, and 13, containing many poor, likewise comprises No. 12, and the greater part of No. 8, in which the poor inhabitants are relatively much less numerous.

We have subjoined a table exhibiting the population of each of the police divisions, according to the last census, and arranged in the four sections visited by the overseers of the poor, so as to exhibit their relative population.

Newtown.		*Ancoats.*		*Central.*		*Portland Street.*	
No. 2..	25581	No. 1..	31573	No. 5 ..	7275	No. 3 ..	11431
$\frac{3}{5}$ of 4..	9337$\frac{4}{5}$	$\frac{2}{5}$ of 4..	6225$\frac{1}{5}$	6 ..	1274	7 ..	9784
				9 ..	3318	$\frac{3}{4}$ of 8 ..	2058
				10 ..	3886	12 ..	1859
				11 ..	13635	13 ..	7269
				14 ..	6834		
				$\frac{1}{4}$ of 8 .	686		
	34918$\frac{4}{5}$		37798$\frac{1}{5}$		36908		32401

The cases relieved at the Churchwardens' offices are classed as Irish and English cases: the first consist exclusively of Irish cases *without settlements*, but under the denomination of English cases, are included *all who have obtained settlements, whether English or Irish;* and this class comprises a very great proportion of Irish. We have been enabled, by the liberality of the Churchwardens, and Mr. Gardiner's politeness, to obtain returns of the relative proportion of these cases during the four winter months of the four years from 1827 to 1831 inclusive. The general table is inserted in the appendix,* but from this we have deduced some more minutely classified results, which we conceive strongly to corroborate the opinions which we have hazarded, concerning the origin and growth of pauperism.

The table contained in the Appendix exhibits, in the first place, an alarming increase of pauperism in

* See Appendix No. 1.

the whole township. The total number of *cases* (each representing, on the average, two and a half individuals) relieved in the township, in the months of November, December, January, and February of 1827 and 28, was 30,717, or included 76,792 individual acts of relief, each continued for an indefinite period. This number had, in the same months of 1830-31, increased to 45,842, or, at a period when the population amounted to 142,026, it included 114,605 individual acts of relief, each of which comprised indefinite portions of the four months, or had *almost doubled in four years.* Supposing these acts to have been administered at all times to different persons, then, more than four-fifths of the whole population were relieved for an indefinite portion of the four winter months.

The relative proportion of Irish cases without settlements, and of English and Irish cases with settlements, and their relative increase during these four years, are perhaps still more remarkable.

DISTRICTS.	*Nov. Dec. Jan. & Feb. of* 1827-8,		1828-9,		1829-30,		1830-31.	
	Irish.	*English.*	*Irish*	*English.*	*Irish*	*English.*	*Irish*	*English.*
NEWTOWN. No. 2 & $\frac{3}{5}$ No. 4	1559	6059	1490	5434	3911	8023	4051	9129
ANCOATS. No. 1 & $\frac{2}{5}$ No. 4	1482	6701	2155	7158	2690	8022	3818	9027
CENTRAL. Nos. 5, 6, 9, 10, 11, 14, & $\frac{1}{4}$ No. 8	366	7422	532	7161	742	9668	909	10214
PORTLAND ST. Nos. 3, 7, 12, 13, and $\frac{3}{4}$ of No 8	264	6864	577	6974	1186	8591	1114	7580

The proportion of Irish cases *without settlements*, in the Ancoats and Newtown Divisions, containing Nos. 1, 2, and 4, and its relative increase, are exceedingly greater than in the Central and Portland Street Districts; notwithstanding that the number of Irish in these latter sections is much augmented by the inclusion of Nos. 3, 7, 10, and 13.

By the following table, this increase may be more easily compared.

DISTRICTS.	*Nov. Dec. Jan. and Feb. of* 1827-8,		1828-9,		1829-30,		1830-31.	
	Irish.	*English.*	*Irish.*	*English.*	*Irish.*	*English.*	*Irish.*	*English.*
NEWTOWN AND ANCOATS.	3041	12760	3645	12592	6601	16045	7869	18156
CENTRAL AND PORTLAND ST.	630	14286	1109	14136	1928	18259	2023	17794

The Newtown and Ancoats Districts have always contained a greater proportion of Irish than any other portion of the town; but the increase of pauperism in the Central and Portland Districts, must evidently be ascribed to the recent rapid colonization of Irish in Divisions 3, 7, and 10; since, whilst the Irish cases, having no *settlements*, have increased from 600 to 2,000, or are more than trebled,—the cases having settlements, which have been relieved, have only increased from 14,000 to 17,000, or about two-ninths. In the same period, the rapid relative increase of the Irish cases having *no settlements*, in the Newtown and Ancoats Districts, renders it extremely probable, that the increase of those cases which *have obtained settlements,* is in a great measure to be imputed to the Irish; and that pauperism, therefore, spreads most rapidly, in an ignorant and demoralized population. These tables also abundantly testify, that *pauperism chiefly prevails in those portions of the town, where the sources and evidences of moral and physical depression, to which we have alluded, are the most numerous.*

The relative proportion of the population to the cases and individuals relieved, in the four Sections visited by the Overseers, is displayed in the following table.

DISTRICTS	Cases relieved for indefinite periods of the four winter months, 1830-31.	POPULATION.	Individual acts of relief for indefinite periods of time.
NEWTOWN..	13180	$34918\frac{4}{5}$ of which $\frac{2}{5}=13967\frac{1}{5}$	32950
ANCOATS....	12890	$37798\frac{1}{5}$ .. $\frac{1}{3}=12599\frac{2}{5}$	32225
Total....	26070	72717 .. $\frac{3}{8}=27143\frac{7}{8}$	65175
CENTRAL ..	11123	36908 .. $\frac{3}{10}=11072\ \frac{4}{10}$	$27807\frac{1}{2}$
PORTLAND..	8694	32401 .. $\frac{1}{4} = 8100$	21735
Total....	19817	69309	49542

The following table* shows the relative proportion of cases relieved in the four Overseers' Sections during three portions of the year 1830-31, each containing four months.

DISTRICTS.	Nov. Dec. Jan. Feb.		March, April, May, June.		July, Aug. Sept. Oct.	
	Irish.	*English.*	*Irish.*	*English.*	*Irish.*	*English.*
NEWTOWN..	4051	9129	3896	7958	3409	7996
ANCOATS...	3818	9027	3333	7801	3280	8107
CENTRAL..	909	10214	815	9474	695	9287
PORTLAND..	1114	7580	897	7050	863	7766
	9892	35950	8941	32283	8247	33156

* See Appendix No. 2.

The population of the township is 142,026; *and the acts of parochial relief in one year,* each continued through indefinite periods of time, *were* 321,172, of which acts 67,700 *concernedIrish who had obtained no settlements.*

The sources of vice and physical degradation are allied with the causes of pauperism. Amongst the poor, the most destitute are too frequently the most demoralized—virtue is the surest economy—vice is haunted by profligacy and want. Where there are most paupers, the gin shops, taverns, and beer houses are most numerous. The following table enumerates the taverns of the town. Gin shops are held under the same licence, and are attached to three fourths of these establishments.

NO. OF LICENSED TAVERN AND INNKEEPERS IN THE TOWNSHIP OF MANCHESTER.

No.		No.		No.	
1	62	6	39	11	37
2	44	7	19	12	16
3	48	8	10	13	25
4	31	9	36	14	13
5	46	10	4		
				Total	430

To this number may perhaps be added 322 gin shops. These last establishments especially abound in the poorest and most destitute districts, where their proportion to the taverns is at least four fifths. We were unable to procure, from the officers of excise in Manchester, information concerning the relative proportion of the beer houses in the several divisions of the town; but we are informed by Mr. Shawcross, of the Police department, that their number is at least three hundred. If we subtract fifty respectable inns, which, however, have generally tap rooms attached to them, one thousand haunts of intemperance exist in Manchester.

The districts 1, 2, 3, and 4, may be conceived to represent most correctly the exclusively labouring population; but in estimating the relative number of all these sources of vice frequented by the population of these districts, it is necessary to include those of the adjoining divisions 5 and 6, where a much smaller proportion of poor resides. The result is, that in Nos. 1, 2, 3, 4, 5, and 6, there are 270 taverns, 216 gin shops, (estimated as four fifths of taverns,) 188 beer houses, (estimated as being distributed through the divisions of the town in the same ratio as the taverns,) total, 674, or more than two thirds of the whole number of taverns, gin shops, and beer houses of the town, may therefore be considered as chiefly ministering to the vicious propensities of the inhabitants of Nos. 1, 2, 3, and 4. Some idea may be formed of the influence of these establishments on the health and morals of the people, from the following statement; for which we are indebted to Mr. Braidley, the Boroughreeve. He observed the number of persons entering a gin shop in five minutes, during eight successive Saturday evenings, and at various periods from seven o'clock until ten. The average result was, 112 men and 163 women, or 275 in forty minutes, which is equal to 412 per hour.

The report of the Committee on gaols reveals the gross mismanagement of the licence system in London, and shews that taverns are the rendezvous of criminals and profligates of the lowest order. The scenes of depravity which occur in them, without the shadow of concealment—the constant temptations to moral errors which they unblushingly offer to those orders of society, which have the least power of repelling them—the seductions to grosser sins by which they enthral the idle and unwary—the maxims of iniquity, and the arts of dishonesty, which are undisguisedly taught in them, by the miscreants who find a daily shelter there—all these glaring abuses demand the prompt and energetic interference of authority with the regulations of establishments, which, without the pretence of necessity, or the veil of one virtuous amusement, are public schools of vice.

The decency of our towns is violated, even in this respect, that every street blazons forth the invitations of these haunts of crime. Gin shops and beer houses encouraged by the law (which seems to value rather the amount of the public revenue, than the prevalence of private virtue) and taverns, over which the police can at present exercise but an imperfect controul, have multiplied with such rapidity that they will excite the strong remonstrances which every lover of good order is prepared to make with government, against the permission, much less the sanction, of such public enormities. Two physicians of great experience who practise in two of our largest manufacturing towns, inform us, that delirium tremens (a disease occasioned by continued intemperance) has increased, within the sphere of their observation, in an alarming ratio since the passing of the Beer-act; and another, who superintends one of the largest public Lunatic Asylums in the provinces, discovers that one great cause of the prevalence of insanity of late years is an addiction to the use of ardent spirits.

The amount of crime is one chief means of ascertaining the moral condition of a community. To the perfection of this estimate it is, however, essential that crimes committed against the person should be distinguished from those against property. *" The moral guilt of the latter depending considerably upon the equality of the distribution of wealth throughout the country, the degree of ease in which the people live ought also to be brought into view; and when we compare the criminal calendars of different nations, we ought not to omit to refer to their respective modes of administering justice, and to the attention paid in each country to that branch of it which we call preventive. That *prevention* is by far the more important care, in point both of duty and expediency, is a truth which governments are beginning to perceive; though in most countries repression, and in not a few vindictiveness,† still form the spirit of the penal code." "So long as the will

* Foreign Quarterly Review, vol. v. p. 404.

† Works of Charles Lucas—*also* "De la Justice de la Prévoyance" —*and* "De la Mission de la Justice Humaine." *Par M. Depêctiaux.*

of man is free, and it is in his power either to conform to the law, or to violate it, the care of the legislature should be to turn that will into the right channel."

The state of the registers, required for an accurate investigation of the amount of crime committed in Manchester, was such as to demand more time in their classification, than, under the circumstances in which this pamphlet was prepared, we were able to give the subject. We have obtained, however, an account of the number of persons committed at the New Bailey Court House, Salford, for the different offences under which their commitment is recorded. The amount of crime exhibited in this table results therefore from a much greater population than that contained in the township; the out-townships being also included, or a population of at least 240,000.

	1829	1830	1831	*Total*
Number of Felons	580	559	638	1777
Persons committed for want of sureties to keep the peace—non-payment of fines—neglect of family, &c.	819	960	996	2775
For want of sureties to appear at the Sessions.	192	153	182	527
For disobeying orders in Bastardy	174	151	181	506
Rogues and Vagabonds	620	743	835	2198
				7713

We subjoin, in a note, a table extracted from a very valuable pamphlet published by Mr. Ridgway, entitled "An Enquiry into the State of the Manufacturing Population, and the Causes and Cures of the

Evils therein existing,"* by which the reader may be enabled to form a more accurate opinion concerning the relative extent to which crime prevails in Manchester.

There is, however, a licentiousness capable of corrupting the whole body of society, like an insidious disease, which eludes observation, yet is equally fatal in its effects. Criminal acts may be statistically classed—the victims of the law may be enumerated —but the number of those affected with the moral leprosy of vice cannot be exhibited with mathematical precision. Sensuality has no record,† and the relaxation of social obligations may coexist with a half dormant, half restless impulse to rebel against all the preservative principles of society; yet these chaotic elements may long smoulder, accompanied only by partial eruptions of turbulence or crime.

---

*1827. | 1827.

Manufacturing Counties.	Population	Crime	Crime to Population 1 to	Agricultural Counties.	Population.	Crime	Crime to Population, 1, to
Cheshire	304,130	497	612	Berkshire....	143,400	208	690
Lancashire ..	1,226,600	2459	495	Essex	319,400	451	708
Middlesex ...	1,295,100	3381	353	Hertford	144,300	205	704
Northumberla	220,500	96	2300	Kent	468,900	632	742
Nottingham. .	206,300	298	695	Hampshire ..	314,000	341	920
Stafford	378,600	569	665	Westmoreland	55,800	20	2790
Warwick....	310,500	602	515	Wiltshire....	245,000	365	671
York	1,321,600	1223	1080	Devonshire ..	484,200	432	1121

Average............ 840......................... 1,043

† No record exists by which the number of illegitimate births can be ascertained. Even this evidence would form a very imperfect rule by which to judge of the comparative prevalence of sensuality.

In the absence of direct evidence, we are unwilling that any statements should rest on our personal testimony; but we again refer with confidence to that of an intelligent and impartial observer.*

One other characteristic of the social body, in its present constitution, appears to us too remarkable and important to be entirely overlooked.

Religion is the most distinguished and ennobling feature of civil communities. Natural attributes of the human mind appear to ensure the culture of some form of worship; and as society rises through its successive stages, these forms are progressively developed, from the grossest observances of superstition, until the truths and dictates of revelation assert their rightful supremacy.

The absence of religious feeling, the neglect of all religious ordinances, affords substantive evidence of so great a moral degradation of the community, as to ensure a concomitant civic debasement. The social body cannot be constructed like a machine, on abstract principles which merely include physical motions, and their numerical results in the production of wealth. The mutual relation of men is not merely dynamical, nor can the composition of their forces be subjected to a purely mathematical calculation. Political economy, though its object be to ascertain the means of increasing the wealth of nations, cannot accomplish its design, without at the

* "Inquiry into the State of the Manufacturing Population." p. 24. *Ridgway.*

same time regarding their happiness, and as its largest ingredient the cultivation of religion and morality.

With unfeigned regret, we are therefore constrained to add, that the standard of morality is exceedingly debased, and that religious observances are neglected amongst the operative population of Manchester. The bonds of domestic sympathy are too generally relaxed; and as a consequence, the filial and paternal duties are uncultivated. The artisan has not time to cherish these feelings, by the familiar and grateful arts which are their constant food, and without which nourishment they perish. An apathy benumbs his spirit. Too frequently the father, enjoying perfect health and with ample opportunities of employment, is supported in idleness on the earnings of his oppressed children; and on the other hand, when age and decrepitude cripple the energies of the parents, their adult children abandon them to the scanty maintenance derived from parochial relief.

That religious observances are exceedingly neglected, we have had constant opportunities of ascertaining, in the performance of our duty as Physician to the Ardwick and Ancoats Dispensary, which frequently conducted us to the houses of the poor on Sunday. With rare exceptions, the adults of the vast population of 84,147 contained in Districts Nos. 1, 2, 3, 4, spend Sunday either in supine sloth, in sensuality, or in listless inactivity. A certain portion only of the labouring classes enjoys even healthful recreation on that day, and a very small number frequent the places of worship.

The fruits of external prosperity may speedily be blighted by the absence of internal virtue. With pure religion and undefiled, flourish frugality, forethought, and industry—the social charities which are the links of kindred, neighbours, and societies—and the amenities of life, which banish the jealous suspicion with which one order regards another. In vain may the intellect of man be tortured to devise expedients by which the supply of the necessaries of life may undergo an increase, equivalent to that of population, if the moral check be overthrown. Crime, diseases, pestilence, intestine discord, famine, or foreign war—those agencies which repress the rank overgrowth of a meagre and reckless race—will, by a natural law, desolate a people devoid of prudence and principle, whose numbers constantly press on the limits of the means of subsistence. We therefore regard with alarm the state of those vast masses of our operative population which are acted upon by all other incentives, rather than those of virtue; and are visited by the emissaries of every faction, rather than by the ministers of an ennobling faith.

The present means or methods of religious instruction are, in the circumstances in which our large towns are placed, most evidently inadequate to their end. The labours of some few devoted men—of whom the world is not worthy—in the houses of the poor, are utterly insufficient to produce a deep and permanent moral impression on the people. Some of our laws, as now administered, encourage indigence and vice, and hence arises an increased necessity for the daily exertions of the teachers of religion, to stem that flood of prevailing immorality which threatens to overthrow the best means that political sagacity can devise for the elevation of the people.

The exertions of Dr. Tuckerman, of Boston, in establishing "a ministry for the poor" had been, until very recently, rather the theme of general and deserved praise, than productive of laudable imitation. This ministration is to be effected, chiefly by a visitation of the houses of the poor, and he proposes as its objects, religious instruction, uninfluenced by sectarian spirit or opinions:—the relief of the most pressing necessities of the poor—first by a well regulated charity, and secondarily, by instruction in domestic economy—exhortations to industry—admonition concerning the consequences of vice, and by obtaining work for the deserving and unemployed. The minister should also encourage the education of the children, should prove the friend of the poor in periods of perplexity, and, when the labourer is subdued by sickness, should breathe into his ear the maxims of virtue, and the truths of religion. He might also act as a medium of communication and a link of sympathy, between the higher and lower classes of society. He might become the almoner of the rich, and thus daily sow the seeds of a kindlier relationship than that which now subsists between the wealthy and the destitute. He might also serve as a faithful reporter of the secret miseries which are suffered in the abodes of poverty, unobserved by those to whom he may come to advocate the cause of the abandoned. The prevalence of the principles and the energetic practice of the precepts of christianity, we may hope, will thus ultimately be made to bind together the now hostile elements of society.

The success of Dr. Tuckerman's labours in Boston had, before the commencement of a similar plan in Manchester, given rise to several societies for the Christian instruction of the people in the Metropolis, and in other parts of the kingdom. Six such societies are now in operation in Manchester and its out-townships—five amongst the Independent, and one amongst the Unitarian Dissenters. The objects proposed by these associations and the means by which these objects are prosecuted, may be estimated by the perusal of an extract from the report of that connected with the Mosley-street Independent Chapel, placed in the appendix. But we regret to add that their number is utterly insufficient to affect the habits, of more than a small portion of the population. The vast portions of the town included in the Ancoats, Newtown, and Portland districts, are utterly unoccupied by this beneficent system; and, when it is further observed, that in those districts reside the most indigent and immoral of our poor, it will be at once apparent, what need there is of the immediate extension of the same powerful agency to them.

Having enumerated so many causes of physical depression, perhaps the most direct proof of the extent to which the effect coexists in natural alliance with poverty, may be derived from the records of the medical charities of the town. During the year preceding July, 1831---21,196 patients were treated at the Royal Infirmary---472 at the House of Recovery---3163 at the Ardwick and Ancoats Dispensary, of which (subtracting one sixth as belonging to the township of Ardwick) 2636 were inhabitants of Manchester---perhaps 2000 at the Workhouse Dispensary, and 1,500 at the Children's---making a total of 27,804, without including the Lock Hospital and the Eye Institution. "If to this sum,"* says Mr. Roberton, engaged in making a similar calculation, "we were further to add the incomparably greater amount of all ranks visited or advised as private patients by the whole body (not a small one) of professional men; those prescribed for by chemists and druggists, scarcely of inferior pretension; and by herb doctors and quacks; those who swallow patent medicines; and lastly the subjects of that ever flourishing branch---domestic medicine; we should be compelled to admit that not fewer, perhaps, than three fourths of the inhabitants of Manchester annually are, or fancy they are, under the necessity of submitting to medical treatment."

* "Remarks on the Health of English Manufacturers, and on the need which exists for the Establishment of Convalescents' Retreats." By J. Roberton.

Ingenious deductions, by Mr. Roberton, from facts contained in the records of the Lying-in Hospital of Manchester, prove, in a different manner, the extreme dependence of the poor, on the charitable institutions of the town. The average annual number of births, (deduced from a comparison of the last four years,) attended by the officers of the Lying-in Charity, is four thousand three hundred; and the number of births to the population may be assumed as one in twenty-eight inhabitants. This annual average of births, therefore, represents a population of 124,400, and assuming that of Manchester and the environs to be 230,000, more than one-half of its inhabitants are therefore either so destitute or so degraded, as to require the assistance of public charity, in bringing their offspring into the world.

The children thus adopted by the public are often neglected by their parents. The early age at which girls are admitted into the factories, prevents their acquiring much knowledge of domestic economy; and even supposing them to have had accidental opportunities of making this acquisition, the extent to which women are employed in the mills, does not, even after marriage, permit the general application of its principles. The infant is the victim of the system; it has not lived long, ere it is abandoned to the care of a hireling or a neighbour, while its mother pursues her accustomed toil. Sometimes a little girl has the charge of the child, or even of two or three collected from neighbouring houses. Thus abandoned to one whose sympathies are not interested in its welfare, or whose time is too often also occupied in household drudgery, the child is ill-fed, dirty, ill-clothed, exposed to cold and neglect; and in consequence, more than one-half of the offspring of the poor (as may be proved by the bills of mortality of the town) die before they have completed their fifth year. The strongest survive; but the same causes which destroy the weakest, impair the vigour of the more robust; and hence the children of our manufacturing population are proverbially pale and sallow, though not generally emaciated, nor the subjects of disease. We cannot subscribe to those exaggerated and unscientific accounts of the physical ailments to which they are liable, which have been lately revived with an eagerness and haste equally unfriendly to taste and truth; but we are convinced that the operation of these causes, continuing unchecked through successive generations, would tend to depress the health of the people; and that consequent physical ills would accumulate in an unhappy progression.

Before the age when, according to law, children can be admitted into the factories, they are permitted to run wild in the streets and courts of the town, their parents often being engaged in labour and unable to instruct them. Five infant schools have been established in Manchester and the suburban townships, in which six hundred children (a miserable portion of those who are of age to learn) receive instruction. "In Britain and Ireland, all sects and all parties approve of infant schools; in France, those who are best qualified to form a judgment, fully appreciate their value, and public tranquillity is alone wanted to secure the universal adoption of them in that country: in Geneva, they are received so zealously as to have become improved by the systematic addition of gardens, in which the children pass more hours than in the school-room; in North America they are gaining ground with the rapidity and steadiness with which everything prospers in the United States: and the republicans of the West, abandoning a deeply rooted and barbarous prejudice, are in some places even providing infant schools for their young slaves. At the Cape of Good Hope the just union of the white and coloured races is begun, not more by the newly imparted equality of rights, than by these establishments being opened in common to the offspring of both; they are in like manner begun to be offered to all classes without invidious distinction in India; and in the *Ultima Thule* of civilization New South Wales, the innocent children of both the convict and the free are, in some measure, rescued by infant schools, from abominations which affect the young, in a manner to which our distance from the scene renders us careless."* The importance of this system, to our large manufacturing towns, is such that we hope funds will be speedily granted by government, so that it may be extended, until all the children of the poor

* Westminster Review, No. xxxiv.

are rescued from ignorance, and from the effects of that bad example, to which they are now subjected in the crowded lanes of our cities.

With a general system of education, we hope will also be introduced institutions, in which the young females of the poor may be instructed in Domestic Economy, and where those pernicious traditional prejudices, which, combined with neglect, occasion the great mortality of their children, may be removed, and they may receive wholesome advice concerning their duties as wives and mothers.

We have avoided alluding to evidence which is founded on general opinion, or depends merely on matters of perception; and have chiefly availed ourselves of such as admitted of a statistical classification. We may, however, be permitted to add, that our own experience, confirmed by that of those members of our profession, on whose judgment we can rely with the greatest confidence, induces us to conclude, that diseases assume a lower and more chronic type in Manchester, than in smaller towns and in agricultural districts; and a residence in the Hospitals of Edinburgh, and practice in its Dispensaries amongst the most debased part of its inhabitants, enables us to affirm, with confidence, that the diseases occurring here admit of less active antiphlogistic or depletory treatment, than those incident to the degraded population of the old town of that city.

Frequent allusion has been made to the supposed rate of mortality in Manchester, as a standard by which the health of the manufacturing population may be ascertained. From the mortality of towns, however, their comparative health cannot be invariably deduced. There is a state of physical depression which does not terminate in fatal organic changes, which, however, converts existence into a prolonged disease, and is not only compatible with life, but is proverbially protracted to an advanced senility.

The difficulty of obtaining returns of burials, from all the places of interment, in the town and suburbs of Manchester, prevented the estimation of the rate of mortality, when the former edition of this Pamphlet was published. Since that period a parliamentary paper has been published (No. 729,) containing a return of the number of burials, occurring annually in Manchester, from 1821 to 1830; and the Board of Health have obtained returns for the last four years, which are confirmatory of this Parliamentary document. We have, from these returns and the census, constructed a table, showing the mortality of every year from 1821 to 1831, inclusive.

The population, by the census of the townships of Ardwick, Broughton, Cheetham Hill, Chorlton-upon-Medlock, Hulme, Manchester, and Salford, in 1811 was 108,993:—in 1821, it was 152,683:—and in 1831, 224,143; or the increase in the first of these periods was to that of the latter, nearly as 44 parts of 115 are to 71 parts of the same number. Hence, supposing the sources of increase from births and immigration, to remain nearly the same, in the intermediate periods, we obtain a rule to distribute the increase of population between 1821 and 1831. Dividing this period into two equal parts, the rate of increase during the first five years would be 44 of 115 equal parts of the whole increase, or in 1826 the population would be 152683+27369 ($\frac{44}{115}$ of the whole increase) =180052 which+44091 ($\frac{71}{115}$, which ratio is assumed to occur during the second five years,) =224143, the population of the town in 1831. These sums being again distributed by the same rule to half of the first and second cycles of five years, and the products thus obtained, divided by five, a tolerably accurate approximation to the half-yearly increase of the population is obtained. By this rule, the following Table of the annual rate of mortality was constructed.

Year	Interments of Churchmen.	Interments of Dissenters.	Total of Interments.	Population.	Rate of Mortality.
1821	1561	1726	3287	152683	46.45
1822	1285	1044	2329	156663	67.223
1823	1585	3230	4815	160664	33.36
1824	1428	3219	4647	166117	35.74
1825	1398	3530	4928	173083	35.12
1826	1548	3804	5352	180052	33.64
1827	1604	3235	4839	186462	38.53
1828	1615	4106	5721	192874	33.73
1829	1479	3719	5198	201691	38.80
1830	1590	4383	5973	212913	35.64
1331			6736	224143	33.27

Some error appears to have occurred in the returns of interments for the first two years, therefore omitting them, the mean annual rate of interments acting as a divisor on the mean numbers of the population from 1823 to 1831 inclusive, will give an approximation to the mean rate of mortality or 188666 ÷ 5356 = 35.22, the mean rate of the annual mortality of Manchester.

Diseases, we have said, assume in this town a comparatively chronic type ; and *a general prevalence of such maladies* is compatible even with a *low* rate of mortality. Acute diseases (which are eminently fatal) prevail, on the contrary, in a population where the standard of health is high, and attack the most robust and plethoric. Thus, a high rate of mortality may often be observed in a community, where the number of persons affected with disease is small ; and on the other hand, general physical depression may concur with the prevalence of chronic maladies, and yet be unattended with a great proportion of deaths. We have elsewhere discussed the origin and shown the great prevalence of dyspepsia, gastralgia,* enteralgia, and chronic bronchitis and phthisis,† in Manchester ; and this reference to the subject may therefore be sufficient here.

The preceding statements must, we fear, be received as valid evidence that many sources of physical depression exist in Manchester. The Special Board of Health, in the course of their inquiries, discovered that they possessed very limited means of removing the evils whose existence was ascertained

* Second Number of the North of England Medical and Surgical Journal: On Gastralgia and Enteralgia.

† Third Number of the North of England Medical and Surgical Journal.

by the reports of the District Inspectors. Some thousands of houses were whitewashed. Several additional gangs of scavengers were employed; and the result of their operations was evident in the improved condition of the public thoroughfares of the town: but to repair and sewer the unpaved streets, courts, &c., and to remove the gross accumulations of filth which they contain, would have entailed upon the town an expenditure for which the fiscal authorities were unwilling to become responsible. Letters were also addressed to the landlords of all houses reported to be out of repair, and of those in which the soughs required repair—which were damp—ill ventilated—or which had no privies, informing them of the defects reported, and requesting them to assist the Special Board in their efforts to ameliorate the physical condition of the poor, by remedying these evils. The disease of the body politic is not superficial, and cannot be cured, or even temporarily relieved, by any specific: its sources are unfortunately remote, and the measures necessary to the removal of its disorders include serious questions on which great difference of opinion prevails.

Visiting Manchester, the metropolis of the commercial system, a stranger regards with wonder the ingenuity and comprehensive capacity, which, in the short space of half a century, have here established the staple manufacture of this kingdom. He beholds with astonishment the establishments of its merchants

—monuments of fertile genius and successful design: —the masses of capital which have been accumulated by those who crowd upon its mart, and the restless but sagacious spirit which has made every part of the known world the scene of their enterprise. The sudden creation of the mighty system of commercial organization which covers this county, and stretches its arms to the most distant seas, attests the power and the dignity of man. Commerce, it appears to such a spectator, here gathers in her storehouses the productions of every clime, that she may minister to the happiness of a favoured race.

When he turns from the great capitalists, he contemplates the fearful strength only of that multitude of the labouring population, which lies like a slumbering giant at their feet. He has heard of the turbulent riots of the people—of machine breaking —of the secret and sullen organization which has suddenly lit the torch of incendiarism, or well nigh uplifted the arm of rebellion in the land. He remembers that political desperadoes have ever loved to tempt this population to the hazards of the swindling game of revolution, and have scarcely failed. In the midst of so much opulence, however, he has disbelieved the cry of need.

Believing that the natural tendency of unrestricted commerce, (unchecked by the prevailing want of education, and the incentives afforded by imperfect laws to improvidence and vice,) is to develop the energies of society, to increase the comforts and luxuries of life, and to *elevate the physical condition* of every member of the social body, we have exposed, with a faithful, though a friendly hand, the condition of the lower orders connected with the manufactures of this town, because we conceive that the evils affecting them result *from foreign and accidental causes.* A system, which promotes the advance of civilization, and diffuses it over the world—which promises to maintain the peace of nations, by establishing a permanent international law, founded on the benefits of commercial association, cannot be inconsistent with the happiness of the *great mass of the people.* There are men who believe that the labouring classes are condemned for ever, by an inexorable fate, to the unmitigated curse of toil, scarcely rewarded by the bare necessaries of existence, and often visited by the horrors of hunger and disease—that the heritage of ignorance, labour, and misery, is entailed upon them as an eternal doom. Such an opinion might appear to receive a gloomy confirmation, were we content with the evidence of fact, derived only from the history of uncivilized races, and of feudal institutions. No modern Rousseau now rhapsodises on the happiness of the state of nature. Moral and physical degradation are inseparable from barbarism. The unsheltered, naked savage, starving on food common to the denizens of the wilderness, never knew the comforts contained in the most wretched cabin of our poor.

Civilization, to which feudality is inimical, but which is most powerfully promoted by commerce, surrounds man with innumerable inventions. It has thus a constant tendency to multiply, without limit, the comforts of existence, and that by an amount of labour, at all times undergoing an indefinite diminution. It continually expands the sphere of his relations, from a dependance on his own limited resources, until it has combined into one mighty league, alike the members of communities, and the powers of the most distant regions. The cultivation of the faculties, the extension of knowledge, the improvement of the arts, enable man to extend his dominion over matter, and to minister, not merely to all the exigencies, but to the capricious tastes and the imaginary appetites of his nature. When, therefore, every zone has contributed its most precious stores—science has revealed her secret laws—genius has applied the mightiest powers of nature to familiar use, making matter the patient and silent slave of the will of man —if want prey upon the heart of the people, we may strongly presume that, besides the effects of existing manners, some accidental barrier exists, arresting their natural and rightful supply.

The evils affecting the working classes, *so far from being the necessary results of the commercial system, furnish evidence of a disease which impairs its energies, if it does not threaten its vitality.*

The increase of the manufacturing establishments, and the consequent colonization of the district, have been exceedingly more rapid than the growth of its civic institutions. The eager antagonization of commercial enterprise, has absorbed the attention, and concentrated the energies of every member of the community. In this strife, the remote influence of arrangements has sometimes been neglected, not from the want of humanity, but from the pressure of occupation, and the deficiency of time. Thus, some years ago, the internal arrangements of mills (now so much improved) as regarded temperature, ventilation, cleanliness, and the proper separation of the sexes, &c., were such as to be extremely objectionable. The same cause has, we think, chiefly occasioned the want of police regulations, to prevent the gross neglect of the streets and houses of the poor.

The great and sudden fluctuations to which trade is liable, are often the sources of severe embarrassment. Sometimes the demand for labour diminishes, and its price consequently falls in a corresponding ratio. On the other hand, the existing population has often been totally inadequate to the required production; and capitalists have eagerly invited a supply of labour from distant counties, and the sister kingdom. The colonization of the Irish was thus first encouraged; and has proved one chief source of the demoralization, and consequent physical depression of the people.

The effects of this immigration, even when regarded as a simple economical question, do not merely include an equation of the comparative cheapness of labour; its influence on civilization and morals, as *they tend to affect the production of wealth,* cannot be neglected.

In proof of this, it may suffice to present a picture of the natural progress of barbarous habits. Want of cleanliness, of forethought, and economy, are found in almost invariable alliance with dissipation, reckless habits, and disease. The population gradually becomes physically less efficient as the producers of wealth—morally so from idleness—politically *worthless* as having few desires to satisfy, and *noxious* as dissipators of capital accumulated. Were such manners to prevail, the horrors of pauperism would accumulate. A debilitated race would be rapidly multiplied. Morality would afford no check to the increase of the population: crime and disease would be its only obstacles—the licentiousness which indulges its capricious appetite, till it exhausts its power—and the disease which, at the same moment, punishes crime, and sweeps away a hecatomb of its victims. A dense mass, impotent alike of great moral or physical efforts, would accumulate; children would be born to parents incapable of obtaining the necessaries of life, who would thus acquire, through the mistaken humanity of the law, a new claim for support from the property of the public. They would drag on an unhappy existence, vibrating between the pangs of hunger and the delirium of dissipation—alternately exhausted by severe and oppressive toil, or enervated by supine sloth. Destitution would now prey on their strength, and then the short madness of debauchery would consummate its ruin. Crime which banishes or destroys its victims, and disease and death, are severe but brief natural remedies, which prevent the unlimited accumulation of the horrors of pauperism. Even war and pestilence, when regarded as affecting a population thus demoralized, and politically and physically debased, seem like storms which sweep from the atmosphere the noxious vapours whose stagnation threatens man with death.

Morality is therefore worthy of the attention of the economist, even when considered as simply ministering to the production of wealth. Civilization creates artificial wants, introduces economy, and cultivates the moral and physical capabilities of society. Hence the introduction of an uncivilized race does not tend even primarily to increase the power of producing wealth, in a ratio by any means commensurate with the cheapness of its labour, and may ultimately retard the increase of the fund for the maintenance of that labour. Such a race is useful only as a mass of animal organization, which consumes the smallest amount of wages. The low price of the labour of such people depends, however, on the paucity of their wants, and their savage habits. When they assist the production of wealth, therefore, their barbarous habits and consequent moral depression must form a part of the equation. They are only necessary to a state of commerce *inconsistent* with such a reward for labour as is calculated to maintain the standard of civilization. A few years pass, and they become burdens to a community whose morals and physical power they have depressed; and dissipate wealth which they did not accumulate.

Conscious of the evils resulting from the immigration of Irish, we nevertheless tremble at the thought of applying unmodified poor-laws to Ireland. In England the system of parochial relief has a most prejudicial influence, in chaining redundant labour to a narrow locality, and thus aggravating the pressure of partial ills, and in relaxing those bonds of the social constitution, industry, forethought, and charity.* Much less could the habits of the Irish be corrected by a parliamentary enactment: and to attempt the removal of their misery, by a constant supply of their wants, would be to offer direct encouragement to idleness, improvidence, and dissipation. It would ultimately render every individual dependent on the State, and change Ireland into a vast infirmary, divided into as many wards as there are parishes, whose endowment would swallow up the entire rental of the country. Such a measure, says Mr. Senior, would †"divide Ireland into as many distinct countries as there are parishes, each peopled by a population *ascripta glebæ;* multiplying without fore-

---

* Chalmers's "Christian and Civic Economy of Large Towns."—"Speech before the General Assembly."—"Political Economy." Page 398, &c. &c.

† Letter to Lord Howick on a Legal Provision for the Irish poor, &c., &c., p. 33.

thought; impelled to labour principally by the fear of punishment; drawing allowance for their children, and throwing their parents on the parish; considering wages not a matter of contract but of right; attributing every evil to the injustice of their superiors; and, when their own idleness or improvidence has occasioned a fall of wages, avenging it by firing the dwellings, maiming the cattle, or murdering the persons of the landlords and overseers; combining, in short, the insubordination of the freeman with the sloth and recklessness of the slave."

We believe, however, that an impost on the rental of Ireland, might be applied with advantage in employing its redundant labour in great public works—such as draining bogs, making public roads, canals, harbours, &c., by which the entire available capital of the country would be increased, and the people would be trained in industrious habits, and more civilized manners. England would then cease to be, to the same extent as at present, the receptacle of the most demoralized and worthless hordes of the sister country.

The Irish, who were invited to colonize the country, at a period when the demand for labour was greater than the native population could supply, have suffered more than any other class from the introduction of the power-loom. The state of transition in employment consequent on a new invention, (by which the powers of production are increased, its cost diminished, and the demand for a peculiar kind of labour almost extinguished,) will always be followed by an embarrassment, whose pressure and duration will be determined *cœteris paribus,* by the extent of the market for manufactures. If by the want of commercial treaties—by the imposition of injudicious duties on foreign produce, which provoke jealous retaliation—the existence of arbitrary restrictions and monopolies, the extent of the market for manufactures be diminished, the demand for labour will be confined within the same limits. A new invention will thus be robbed of half its rewards, since we deprive other nations of the power of buying our manufactures, by refusing to accept what they offer in exchange. We depress the spirit of their enterprise; and we discourage our own. The relations of commerce are those of unlimited reciprocity—not of narrow and bigoted exclusion. We encourage genius and industry in proportion as we permit them to receive their reward in the riches of every clime. We dam up not only the well-spring of our own wealth and happiness, but of that of other nations, when we refuse to barter the results of the ingenuity and perseverance of our artisans, for the products of the bounty of other climates, or the arts and genius of other people. Unrestricted commerce, on the other hand, would rapidly promote the advance of civilization, by cultivating the physical and mental power of individuals and nations to multiply the amount of natural products, and to create those artificial staple commodities, by the barter of which they acquire the riches of other regions. Every new invention in agriculture or manufactures—every improvement in the powers of transmission, would enable its possessors, by the same amount of labour, to obtain a greater quantity of foreign products in exchange. The labour of man would be constantly, to an indefinite extent, diminished,* whilst its reward would be, at the same time, perpetually increased. Human power would be employed "in its noblest occupation, that of giving a direction to the mere physical power which it had conquered."†

But under a restrictive system, the demand for the results of labour is limited, not by the wants of the whole world, but of the market from which commodities are received in exchange. Even then, as civilization multiplies the desires, and stimulates the industry and ingenuity of man, the quantity of products permitted to be bartered for our manufactures has a constant tendency to increase. Unfortunately, however, the restrictions which fetter commerce are so numerous, and the monopolies which exclude free trade from the fairest portions of the earth are so extensive, as to render the progressive increase in the demand for the results of our labour and capital slow.

---

* Observations on the Influence of Machinery upon the Working Classes of the Community, By John Kennedy, Esq.: Memoirs of the Literary and Philosophical Society of Manchester, vol. v. second series.—*Also* The Economy of Machinery and Manufactures, By Charles Babbage, Esq.

† Results of Machinery, p. 193.

Population, nevertheless, increases the supply of labour in at least as great a ratio as the demand existing under a restrictive system. Every invention, therefore, which diminishes the quantity of labour necessary to produce the objects of barter, lessens its price, and excludes, for an indefinite period, a great part of the population from employment. By this system the profits of capital are increased, though not in the same ratio as the wages of labour are for a time diminished. But, were the restrictions abolished, each new invention would not only enable man to purchase, by a smaller amount of labour, a larger portion of foreign products, but would, by these means, powerfully stimulate the genius and industry of other nations, whose demand for our manufactures would increase in a ratio at least equal to their accumulation. In other words, improvements in machinery *diminish the cost of production;* but if the demand for manufactures be limited by arbitrary enactments, *the increased employment* which would also be their natural and inevitable result, *is prevented,* until commerce is able, in some other way, to compensate for the evils of injudicious legislation. We have *capital and labour*—but to obtain the greatest amount of commercial advantages, we must also have an *unlimited power of exchange.*

We believe, therefore, that chiefly to *this cause* must be attributed the combined misery of severe labour and want entailed on that wretched but extensive class, the hand-loom weavers of the cotton trade.

Were an unlimited exchange permitted to commerce, the hours of labour might be reduced, and time afforded for the education and religious and moral instruction of the people. With a virtuous population, engaged in free trade, the existence of redundant labour would be an evil of brief duration, rarely experienced. The unpopular, but alas, too necessary proposals of emigration would no longer be agitated. Ingenuity and industry would draw from the whole world a tribute more than adequate to supply the ever increasing demands of a civilized nation.

The duties imposed on the introduction of foreign corn were originally intended, by raising the price of grain, to act as a compensation to the landowner for the supposed unequal pressure of taxation upon him. This inequality of the public burdens has, however, been exceedingly exaggerated, and those taxes, which are said to be derived from land on which corn is grown, are also procured from many other descriptions of property which are not protected. The faults of our present financial system* are so numerous, that if the principle of relieving the inequality of the pressure of taxation be admitted, we must pay back in bounties one third of what is obtained by taxes. The scarcity and dearness of food certainly bring to the agricultural population no benefit, after the brief demand for labour necessary to bring fresh soils into cultivation is past. The landowner alone receives

* Sir H. Parnell, on Financial Reform.

any advantage from the high price of food, and that much less than has generally been supposed. The fluctuating scale by which the duties on corn are at present regulated, has produced the most disastrous effects among the agricultural tenantry: rents have been paid out of capital, and estates have been injured, in consequence of the embarrassments of the cultivators. A tax *on the staple commodity of life* enhances the price of all other food, by increasing the wages of labour, and the rent of land; and, as it enters as an element into the cost of every article produced, (and that in a ratio constantly accumulating with the amount of labour employed,) it presses heavily, though indirectly, on the superior classes, and upon all other consumers. Not the least injurious effects of the present Corn-law, are the burden of supporting an unemployed population, which it entails on society at large, and the insecurity of property which results from the near approach to destitution of a large portion of its members. But since this system simultaneously contracts the market of the capitalist, (by excluding one most important object of barter,) and increases the cost of production, its direst effects are felt in the manufacturing districts, which have long been maintaining an unequal struggle with foreign competitors. In the cotton trade, to the expense of importing the raw material, and that chiefly from one of those countries where bounties on manufactures exist, is added the pressure of one tax, on the raw material, and of another, which, by raising the price of labour, increases that of the manufactured result. Industry, invention, the most subtle sagacity, and the most daring enterprise appear at length almost baffled by the difficulties they encounter. The profits of capital are reduced to the most meagre attenuation—the rapidity of production, of transmission and return, appear to have reached their utmost limit. Injudicious duties on foreign produce have provoked retaliation, and the manufactures of other countries are supported by artificial expedients in rivalry with our own. The difficulty of changing the system is every day increased, until, ere long, it may become a serious question with other countries, whether the advantages to be derived from free trade can compensate for the sacrifice of the capital embarked in their commercial establishments. The cotton manufacture is rapidly spreading all over the continent, and particularly in Switzerland and France; and America threatens us with a more formidable competition.

Under these circumstances, every part of the system appears necessary to the preservation of the whole. The profits of trade will not allow a greater remuneration for labour, and competition even threatens to reduce its price. *Whatever time is subtracted from the hours of labour* must be accompanied with an equivalent deduction from its rewards;* the

---

* The effect of such a measure is thus correctly described in an able and perspicuous pamphlet lately published, entitled "A Letter

restrictions of trade prevent other improvements, and we fear that the condition of the working classes cannot be much improved, until the burdens and restrictions of the commercial system are abolished.

We will yield to none in an earnest and unqualified opposition to the present restrictions and burdens of commerce, and chiefly because they lessen the wages of the lower classes, increase the price of food, and prevent the reduction of the hours of labour :—because they will retard the application of a general and efficient system of education, and thus not merely depress the health, but debase the morals of the poor. Those politicians who propose a serious reduction of the hours of labour, unpreceded by the relief of commercial burdens, seem not to believe that this measure would inevitably depress the wages of the poor, whilst the price of the necessaries of life would con-

---

to Lord Althorp, in Defence of the Cotton Factories of Lancashire, By Holland Hoole."

"If Mr. Sadler's bill becomes a law, the masters will have the choice of two evils. Either they must reduce the hours of labour to the limit proposed to be fixed for children, (fifty eight hours per week) or they must place their establishments without the pale of this enactment, by discharging all persons under eighteen years from their factories."

"In the former case a reduction of the *wages* of all persons employed, whether children or adults, corresponding with the reduction of the time of labour must inevitably take place." "Not a few of the master cotton spinners have determined to adopt the other course above mentioned, namely, to *discharge* from their employment all the hands under eighteen years of age, as soon as the proposed law comes into operation."

tinue the same. They appear, also, not to have sufficiently reflected, that, if this measure *were unaccompanied by a general system of education*, the time thus bestowed, would be wasted or misused. If this depression of wages, coincident with an increase of the time generally spent by an uneducated people, in sloth or dissipation, be carefully reflected upon, the advocates of this measure will, perhaps, be less disposed to regard it as one calculated to confer unqualified benefits on the labouring classes. To retrace the upward path from evil and misery, is difficult. Health is only acquired, after disease, by passing through slow and painful stages. Neither can the evils which affect the operative population be instantly relieved, by the exhibition of any single notable remedy.

Men are, it must be confessed, too apt to regard with suspicion, those who differ from them in opinion, and rancorous animosity is thus engendered between those whose motives are pure, and between whose opinions only shades of difference exist. We believe that no objection to a reduction of the hours of labour would exist, amongst the enlightened capitalists of the cotton trade, if the difficulty of maintaining, under the present restrictions, the commercial position of the country did not forbid it. Were these restrictions abolished, they would cease to fear the competition of their foreign rivals, and the working classes of the community would find them to be the warmest advocates of every measure which could conduce to the physical comfort, or moral elevation of the poor.

A general and efficient system of education would be devised—a more intimate and cordial association would be cultivated between the capitalist and those in his employ—the poor would be instructed in habits of forethought and economy ; and, in combination with these great and general efforts to ameliorate their condition, when the restrictions of commerce had been abolished, a reduction in the hours of labour, would tend to elevate the moral and physical condition of the people.

We are desirous of adding a few observations on each of these measures. Ere the moral and physical condition of the operative population can be much elevated, a system of national education so extensive and liberal as to supply the wants of the whole labouring population must be introduced. Ignorance is twice a curse—first from its necessarily debasing effects, and then because rendering its victim insensible to his own fate, he endures it with supine apathy. The ignorant are, therefore, properly, the care of the state. Our present means of instruction are confined to Sunday Schools, and a few Lancasterian and National Schools, quite inadequate to the wants of the population. The absence of education is like that of cultivation, the mind untutored becomes a waste, in which prejudices and traditional errors grow as rankly as weeds. In this sphere of labour, as in every other, prudent and diligent culture is necessary to obtain genial products from the soil; noxious agencies are abroad, and, while we refuse to sow the germs of truth and virtue, the winds of heaven bring the winged seeds of error and vice. Moreover, as education is delayed, a stubborn barrenness affects the faculties—want of exercise renders them inapt—he that has never been judiciously instructed, has not only to master the first elements of truth, and to unlearn error, but in proportion as the period has been delayed, will be the difficulty of these processes. What wonder then that the teachers of truth should make little impression on an unlettered population, and that the working classes should become the prey of those *who flatter their passions, adopt their prejudices, or even descend to imitate their manners.*

If a period ever existed, when public peace was secured, by refusing knowledge to the population, that epoch has lapsed. The policy of governments may have been little able to bear the scrutiny of the people. This may be the reason why the fountains of English literature have been sealed—and the works of our reformers, our patriots, and our confessors—the exhaustless sources of all that is pure and holy, and of good report, amongst us—*have not been made accessible and familiar to the poor.* Yet, literature of this order is destined to determine the structure of our social constitution, and to become the mould of our national character; and they who would dam up the flood of truth from the lower ground, cannot prevent its silent transudation. A little knowledge is thus inevitable, and it is proverbially a dangerous thing. Alarming disturbances of social order generally commence with *a people only partially instructed.* The preservation of *internal peace,* not less than the improvement of our national institutions, depends on the education of the working classes.

Government unsupported by popular opinion, is deprived of its true strength, and can only retain its power by the hateful expedients of despotism. Laws which obtain not general consent are dead letters, or obedience to them must be purchased by blood. But ignorance perpetuates the prejudices and errors which contend with the just exercise of a legitimate authority, and makes the people the victims of those ill-founded panics which convulse society, or seduces them to those tumults which disgrace the movements of a deluded populace. Unacquainted with the real sources of their own distress, misled by the artful misrepresentations of men whose element is disorder, and whose food faction can alone supply, the people have too frequently neglected the constitutional expedients by which redress ought only to have been sought, and have brought obloquy on their just cause, by the blind ferocity of those insurrectionary movements, in which they have assaulted the institutions of society. That good government may be stable, the people must be so instructed, that they may love that *which they know to be right.*

The present age is peculiarly calculated to illustrate the truth of these observations. When we have equally to struggle against the besotted idolatry of ancient modes, which would retain error, and the headlong spirit of innovation, which, under the pretence of reforming, would destroy—now, hurried wildly onwards to the rocks on which we may be crushed; and then, sucked back into the sullen deep, where we fear to be whelmed—between this Scylla and that Charybdis, shall we hesitate to guide the vessel of the state, by the power of an enlightened popular opinion! The increase of intelligence and virtue amongst the mass of the people, will prove our surest safeguard, in the absence of which, the possessions of the higher orders might be, to an ignorant and brutal populace, like the fair plains of Italy, to the destroying Vandal. The wealth and splendor, the refinement and luxury of the superior classes, might provoke the wild inroads of a marauding force, before whose desolating invasion, every institution which science has erected, or humanity devised, might fall, and beneath whose feet all the arts and ornaments of civilized life might be trampled with ruthless violence.

Even our national power rests on this basis, which power is sustained *" not so much by the number of the people, as by the ability and character of that people;" and we should tremble to behold the excellent brightness and terrible form of a great nation, resting, like the 'image' of the prophet, on a population,

* Cobbett's Cottage Economy. Introduction.

in which the elements of strength and weakness are so commingled, as to ensure the dissolution of every cohesive principle, in that portion of society, which is thus not inaptly portrayed by the feet which were part of iron and part of clay.

The education afforded to the poor must be substantial. The mere elementary rudiments of knowledge are chiefly useful, as a means to an end. The poor man will not be made a much better member of society, by being only taught to read and write. His education should comprise such branches of general knowledge, as would prove sources of rational amusement, and would thus elevate his tastes above a companionship in licentious pleasures. Those portions of the exact sciences which are connected with his occupation, should be familiarly explained to him, by popular lectures, and *cheap treatises.* To this end, Mechanics' Institutions (partly conducted by the artisans themselves, in order that the interest they feel in them may be constantly excited and maintained) should be multiplied by the patrons of education, among the poor. The ascertained truths of political science should be early taught to the labouring classes, and *correct* political information should be constantly and industriously disseminated amongst them. Were the taxes on periodical publications removed, men of great intelligence and virtue might be induced to conduct journals, established for the express purpose of directing to legitimate objects that restless activity by which the people are of late agitated. Such works, sanctioned by the names of men distinguished for their sagacity, spirit, and integrity, would command the attention and respect of the working classes. The poor might thus be also made to understand their political position in society, and the duties that belong to it—"that* they are in a great measure the architects of their own fortune; that what others can do for them is trifling indeed, compared with what they can do for themselves; that they are infinitely more interested in the preservation of public tranquillity than any other class of society; that mechanical inventions and discoveries are always supremely advantageous to them; and that their real interests can only be effectually promoted, by displaying greater prudence and forethought." They should be instructed in the nature of their domestic and social relations. The evils which imprudent marriages entail on those who contract them, on their unhappy offspring, and on society at large, should be exhibited in the strongest light. The consequences of idleness, improvidence, and moral deviations, should be made the subjects of daily admonition; so that a young man might enter the world, not, as at present, without chart or compass, blown hither and thither by every gust of passion, but, with a perfect knowledge of the dangers to which he is exposed, and of the way to escape them.

---

* McCulloch, on the rise, progress, and present state of the British Cotton Manufacture. Edinburgh Review, No. 91.

The relation between the capitalist and those in his employ, might prove a fruitful source of the most beneficial comments. The misery which the working classes have brought upon themselves, by their mistaken notions on this subject, is incalculable, not to mention the injury which has accrued to capitalists, and to the trade of this country.

Much good *would result from a more general and cordial association of the higher and lower orders. In Liverpool a charitable society exists denominated the "Provident," whose members include a great number of the most influential inhabitants. The town is subdivided into numerous districts, the inspection and care of each of which is committed to one or two members of the association. They visit the people in their houses—sympathize with their distresses, and minister to the wants of the necessitous; but above all, they acquire by their charity, the right of inquiring into their arrangements—of instructing them in domestic economy—of recommending sobriety, cleanliness, forethought, and method.

Every capitalist might contribute much to the happiness of those in his employ, by a similar exercise of enlightened charity. He might establish provident associations and libraries amongst his people. Cleanliness, and a proper attention to clothing and

* An Address to the Higher Classes on the present State of Feeling among the Working Classes.

diet* might be enforced. He has frequent opportunities of discouraging the vicious, and of admonishing the improvident. By visiting the houses of the operatives, he might advise the multiplication of household comforts and the culture of the domestic sympathies. Principle and interest admonish him to receive none into his employ, unless they can produce the most satisfactory attestations to their character.

Above all he should provide instruction for the children of his workpeople: he should stimulate the appetite for useful knowledge, and supply it with appropriate food.

Happily, the effect of such a system is not left to conjecture. In large towns serious obstacles oppose its introduction; but in Manchester more than one enlightened capitalist confesses its importance, and has made preparations for its adoption. In the country, the facilities are greater; and many establishments might be indicated, which exhibit the results of combined benevolence and intelligence. One example may suffice.

Twelve hundred persons are employed in the factories of Mr. Thomas Ashton, of Hyde. This gentleman has erected commodious dwellings for his workpeople, with each of which he has connected every convenience that can minister to comfort. He resides in their immediate vicinity, and has frequent

---

* True Theory of Rent, By T. Perronnet Thomson, Esq.

opportunities of maintaining a cordial association with his operatives. Their houses are well furnished, clean, and their tenants exhibit every indication of health and happiness. Mr. Ashton has also built a school, where 640 children, chiefly belonging to his establishment, are instructed on Sunday, in reading, writing, arithmetic, &c. A library, connected with this school, is eagerly resorted to, and the people frequently read after the hours of labour have expired. An infant school is, during the week, attended by 280 children, and in the evenings others are instructed by masters selected for the purpose. The factories themselves are certainly excellent examples of the cleanliness and order which may be attained, by a systematic and persevering attention to the habits of the artisans.

The effects of such enlightened benevolence may be, to a certain extent, exhibited by statistical statements. The population, before the introduction of machinery, chiefly consisted of colliers, hatters, and weavers. Machinery was introduced in 1801, and the following table exhibits its consequences in the augmentation of the value of property, the diminution of poor rates, and the rapid increase of the amount assessed for the repairs of the highway, during a period, in which the population of the township increased from 830 to 7138.—

Township of Hyde, in the Parish of Stockport, in the County of Chester.

Year.	Estimated value of property assessable to the Poor's Rate.		Sums assessed for the Relief of the Poor.			Sums assessed for the Repairs of the Highway.			Population	REMARKS.
	£.	s.	£.	s.	d.	£.	s.	d.		
1801	693	10	533	12	0	2	11	6	830	Machinery introduced.
2	697	0	394	19	4	51	19	5		
3	697	0	336	8	0	52	3	0¾		
4	697	10	325	10	0	52	5	9¾		
5	724	0	385	17	4	100	6	11½		
6	786	0	339	6	0	110	12	11½		
7	829	0	276	6	8	172	7	9½		
8	898	10	223	1	4	177	6	10		
9	915	0	286	16	8	152	17	9		
1810	935	0	345	10	0	146	18	3½		
1	945	10	417	6	4	199	19	3½	1806	
2	975	15	471	8	4	168	11	1		Riots, Machinery broken in various places. Power Looms introduced.
3	986	0	687	7	8	148	18	11¼		
4	997	0	630	6	8	144	18	8¼		
5	1029	15	508	18	0	99	9	3½		
6	1079	5	390	2	0	156	9	5¼		
7	1109	15	502	3	6	150	2	8½		
8	1142	0	421	2	0	171	15	9		
9	1242	0	431	6	0	201	8	7½		
1820	1272	0	355	4	8	229	11	7		
1	1371	15	274	7	0	265	1	1	3355	New County Rate made: from this time the County Rate, together with the salary of the serving officer, average £200. per annum.
2	1429	5	435	10	6	440	12	0¾		
3	1570	0	479	8	0	454	8	8¾		
4	1792	0	348	17	0	506	2	2½		
5	1957	0	398	11	0	524	19	3½		
6	2093	10	438	7	6	573	10	7¾		
7	2354	15	479	6	3	598	10	5		
8	2533	0	502	7	4	732	4	3½		
9	2623	0	790	11	9	681	19	6½		
1830	2727	0	549	16	0	578	10	1		
1	2783	0	*834	18	9	359	5	5½	7138	
Total in 31 yrs.			13994	13	7	8405	19	7		
Average......			451	10	0	271	7	2		

* A considerable balance in the Overseer's hands.

This table exhibits a cheering proof of the advantages which may be derived from the commercial system, under judicious management. We feel much confidence in inferring that where so little pauperism exists, the taint of vice has not deeply infected the population; and concerning their health we can speak from personal observation. The rate of mortality, from statements* with which Mr. Ashton has politely

---

* *Minute of Deaths among the Spinners, Piecers and Dressers, employed at the works of Mr. Thomas Ashton, in Hyde, from* 1819 *to* 1832, 13 *years, viz:*—SPINNERS. Rd. Robinson, James Seville, David Cordingly, Eli Taylor. PIECERS. Jas. Rowbotham, Wm. Green. DRESSERS. John Cocker, Samuel Broadhurst.

There are employed at these works 61 rovers and spinners, 120 piecers, and 38 dressers: total 219; among whom there are at this time 10 spinners whose ages are respectively from forty up to fifty six years; and among the dressers there are 12 whose ages are equal to that of the above spinners. We have no orphans at this place, neither have we any family receiving parochial relief; nor can we recollect the time when there was any such. The different clubs or sick lists among the spinners, dressers, overlookers and mechanics employed here, allow ten or twelve shillings per week to the members during sickness, and from six to eight pounds to a funeral; which applies also to the member's wife, and, in some cases, one half or one fourth to the funeral of a child. The greatest amount of contributions to these funds has in no one year exceeded five shillings and sixpence from each member.

The weavers (chiefly young women) have also a funeral club, the contributions to which are fourpence per member to each funeral. In the above period of thirteen years there have happened among them only forty funerals.

Total number of persons employed, twelve hundred, who maintain about two thousand. JOSEPH TINKER, Book-keeper.

Hyde, 27th March, 1832.

furnished us, appears to be exceedingly low. In thirteen years (during the first six of which, the number of rovers, spinners, piecers and dressers was one hundred, and during the last seven, above two hundred) only eight deaths occurred, though the same persons were, with rare exceptions, employed during the whole period. Supposing, for the sake of convenience, that the deaths were nine; then by ascribing three to the first six years, and six to the last seven, the mortality during the former period was one in 200, and during the latter, one in 233. The number of weavers during the first six years was 200, and during the last seven 400; and in this body of workmen 40 deaths occurred in thirteen years. By ascribing thirteen of these deaths to the first six years, and twenty seven to the last seven, the mortality, during the former period, was one in 92, and during the latter, 1 in 103.

These facts indicate that the present hours of labour do not injure the health of a population, *otherwise favourably situated,* but that, when evil results ensue, they must chiefly be ascribed to the combination of this *with other causes of moral and physical depression.*

Capitalists, whose establishments are situated in the country, enjoy many opportunities of controling the habits and ministering to the comforts of those in their employ, which cannot exist in a large manufacturing town. In the former, the land in the vicinity is generally the property of the manufacturer, and upon this he may build commodious houses, and surround the operative with all the conveniences and attractions of a home. In the town, the land is often in the possession of non-resident proprietors, anxious only to obtain the largest amount of chief rent. It is therefore let in separate lots to avaricious speculators, who (unrestrained by any general enactment, or special police regulation) build without plan, wretched abodes in confused groups, intersected by narrow, unpaved or undrained streets and courts. By this disgraceful system the moral and physical condition of the poor undergoes an inevitable depression.

In Manchester *" it is much to be regretted that the surveyors of highways, or some other body of gentlemen specially appointed, were not, forty years ago, invested with authority to regulate the laying out of building-land within the precincts of the town, and to enforce the observance of certain conditions, on the part of the owners and lessees of such property." Private rights ought not to be exercised so as to produce a public injury. The law, which describes and punishes offences against the person and property of the subject, should extend its authority by establishing a social code, in which the rights of communities should be protected from the assaults of partial interests. By exercising its functions in the former case, it does not wantonly interfere with

* Dr. Lyon on the Medical Topography and Statistics of Manchester.—*North of England Medical and Surgical Journal*, vol. i. page 17.

the liberty of the subject, nor in the latter, would it violate the reverence due to the sacred security of property.

The powers obtained by the recent changes in the police act of Manchester are retrospective, and exclusively refer to the removal of existing evils: their application must also necessarily be slow. We conceive that special police regulations should be framed for the purpose of preventing the recurrence of that gross neglect of decency and violation of order, whose effects we have described.

Streets should be built according to plans determined (after a conference with the owners) by a body of commissioners, specially elected for the purpose—their width should bear a certain relation to the size and elevation of the houses erected. Landlords should be compelled, on the erection of any house, to provide sufficient means of drainage, and each to pave his respective area of the street. Each habitation should be provided with a due receptacle for every kind of refuse, and the owner should be obliged to whitewash the house, at least once every year. Inspectors of the state of houses should be appointed: and the repair of all those, reported to be in a state inconsistent with the health of the inhabitants, should be enforced at the expense of the landlords. If the rents of houses are not sufficient to remunerate the owners for this repair, their situation must in general be such, or their dilapidation so extreme, as to render them so undesirable to the comfort, or so prejudicial to the health of the tenants, that they ought no longer to be inhabited.

Sources of physical depression, arising from the neglect of these arrangements, abound to such an extent in Manchester, that it has been sagaciously suggested that some powerful counteracting causes must also be in operation, or we should otherwise frequently be subjected to the visitation of fatal epidemic diseases. What all those causes may be it would perhaps be vain to speculate, but it might be demonstrated that the establishment of the House of Recovery has had a most salutary influence in checking the spread of typhus fever.

The associations of workmen, for protecting the price of labour, have too frequently been so directed, as to occasion increased distress to the operatives, embarrassment to the capitalist, and injury to the trade of the country, whereas, were they properly conducted, they might exercise a generally beneficial influence. No combination can permanently raise the wages of labour, above the limit defined by the relation existing between population and capital; but partial monopolies, and individual examples of oppression might, by this means, be removed, and occasions exist, when, on the occurrence of a fresh demand, the natural advance of the price of labour might be hastened. So long, however, as these associations needlessly provoke animosity, by the slander of private character, by vexatious and useless interference, and by exciting turbulence and alarm, many of their most legitimate purposes cannot be pursued. Distrust will then prevent masters and workmen from framing regulations for their mutual benefit, such as modes of determining the quantity or quality of work produced, and the collection of correct statistical information— or from combining in applications to government for improvements of the laws which affect commerce. Capitalists, fearing combination amongst their workmen, will conceal the true state of the demand, and thus at one period, the operative will be deprived of that reward of his labour, which he would otherwise obtain, and, at another, will receive, no warning of the necessary reduction of manufacturing establishments; which change may thus occur at a period, when, having made no provision for it, he may be least able to encounter the privation of his ordinary means of support. The risks attending the outlay of capital, the extension of the sphere of enterprise, and even the execution of contracts are, by the uncertainty thus introduced into circumstances affecting the supply of labour, exceedingly augmented. Larger stocks must be maintained, less confidence will attend commercial transactions, and an increase of price is necessary to cover these expenses and risks. "* If an establishment consist of several branches which can be only carried on jointly, as, for instance, of iron mines, blast furnaces, and a colliery, in which there are distinct classes of workmen, it becomes necessary

* The Economy of Machinery and Manufactures. By Chas. Babbage, Esq. Page 250.

to keep on hand a larger stock of materials than would otherwise be required, if it were certain that no combinations would arise. The proprietors of one establishment in the trade which has been mentioned, think it expedient always to keep above ground, a supply of coal, for six months, which is in that instance equal in value to about £10,000."

The efforts of these associations have not unfrequently occasioned the introduction of machinery into branches of labour, whence skill has been driven, to undertake the severer and ill rewarded occupation of ordinary toil. When machinery thus *suddenly* excludes skilled labour, much greater temporary distress is occasioned to the operative, than by the natural and gradual progress of mechanical improvements. By employing the power of these associations, at periods when an advance of wages has been impossible, or to resist a fall which the influence of natural causes rendered inevitable, the workmen have not only prevented the accumulation of the fund for the maintenance of labour, at a period when the advance of population was unchecked, but they have dissipated their own savings, as well as the monies of the union, in useless efforts, and, when pride and passion have combined to prolong the struggle, their furniture and clothes have been sold, and their families reduced to the extremes of misery. The effects of these 'strikes' are frequently shared by unwilling sufferers, first, among those whose labour cannot be conducted independently of the body, which has refused to work, and secondly, by those whose personal will is controled, by the threats or the actual violence of the rest. During the 'strike,' habits of idleness or dissipation are not unfrequently contracted—suspicion degenerates into hatred—and a wide gulph is created between the masters and the workmen. The kindlier feelings are extinguished, secret leagues are formed, property is destroyed, such of the operatives as do not join the combination, are daily assaulted, and at length, licence mocks the law with the excesses of popular tumult.

It is impossible that the distrust, thus created, should not sometimes occasion the exclusion from the trade, of the entire body of workmen concerned, and the introduction of a new colony of operatives into the district. The labourers thus immigrating, are not seldom an uncivilized and foreign race, so that, if ever the slightest tendency to cordial co-operation existed between the capitalist and the operative, that is now dissolved. The obstinacy with which this struggle with the manufacturer has sometimes been conducted, has occasioned the removal of establishments to another district, or even to a foreign country, and these contests are always unfavorable to the introduction of fresh capital, into the neighbourhood where they occur.

The more deserving and intelligent portions of the labouring class, are often controled by the greater boldness and activity of that portion which has least knowledge and virtue. Thus, we fear, that the power of the Co-operative Unions has been directed to mischievous objects, and the funds, the time, and energies of the operatives, have been wasted on unfeasible projects. Moreover, they who, as they are the weakest, ought to be, and generally are, the firmest advocates of liberty, have been misled into gross violations of the liberty of their fellow workmen. The power of these unions, to create disorder, or to attain improper objects, would be destroyed, if every assault were prosecuted, or the violation of the liberty of the subject prevented by the assiduous interference of an efficient police. The radical remedy for these evils is such an education as shall teach the people in what consists their true happiness, and how their interests may be best promoted.

The tendency to these excesses would be much diminished, did a cordial sympathy unite the higher with the lower classes of society. The intelligence of the former should be the fountain whence this should flow. If the *results* of labour be solely regarded, in the connexion of the capitalist with those in his employ, the first step is taken towards treating them as a mere animal power necessary to the mechanical processes of manufacture. This is a heartless, if not a degrading association. The contract for the rewards of labour conducted on these principles issues in suspicion, if not in rancorous animosity.

The operative population constitutes one of the most important elements of society, and when numerically considered, the magnitude of its interests and the extent of its power assume such vast proportions, that the folly which neglects them is allied to madness. If the higher classes are unwilling to diffuse intelligence among the lower, those exist who are ever ready to take advantage of their ignorance; if they will not seek their confidence, others will excite their distrust; if they will not endeavour to promote domestic comfort, virtue, and knowledge among them, their misery, vice, and prejudice will prove volcanic elements, by whose explosive violence the structure of society may be destroyed. The principles developed in this Pamphlet, as they are connected with facts occurring within a limited sphere of observation, may be unwittingly supposed to have relation to that locality alone. The object of the author will, however, be grossly misunderstood, if it be conceived, that he is desirous of placing in invidious prominence defects which he may have observed in the social constitution of his own town. He believes the evils here depicted to be incident, in a much larger degree, to many other great cities, and the means of cure here indicated to be equally capable of application there. His object is simply to offer to the public *an example* of what he conceives to be too generally the state of the working classes, throughout the kingdom, and to illustrate by *specific instances*, evils everywhere requiring the immediate interference of legislative authority.

APPENDIX.

TABLE No. 1. p. 28.

INQUIRIES CONCERNING THE STATE OF HOUSES.

District. No.

Name of Street, Court, &c.	*No*	*No.*	*Name of Street, Court, &c.*	*No*	*No.*
1. Is the House in good Repair?			12. Is a private privy attached to the house ?..		
2. Is it clean ?..........			13. Will the tenants assist in cleansing the streets and houses ?		
3. Does it require White-washing ?............					
4. Are the rooms well ventilated, or can they be without change in windows, &c.			14. Will they allow the Town's Authorities to whitewash them, if they cannot conveniently do it themselves ?........		
5. Is the house damp, or dry ?................			15. Are the tenants generally healthy or not ?..		
6. Are the cellars inhabited ?			16. What is their occupation ?		
7. Are these inhabited cellars damp or ever flooded?					
8. Are the soughs in a bad state ?			17. Remarks concerning food, clothing, and fuel.		
9. Who is the proprietor?					
10. What number of families or lodgers does the house contain ?			18. Habits of life.		
11. What is the state of the beds, closets, and furniture ?			19. General Observations.		

TABLE No. 2. P. 28.			
INQUIRIES CONCERNING THE STATE OF STREETS, COURTS, ALLEYS, &c.			
District. No. Inspectors.			
Names of Streets, Courts, Alleys, &c.	*Name*	*Name*	*Name*
Is the street, court, or alley narrow, and is it ill ventilated?			
Is it paved or not?			
If not, is it under the Police Act?			
Does it contain heaps of refuse, pools of stagnant fluid, or deep ruts?			
Are the public and private privies well situated, and properly attended to?			
Is the street, court, or alley, near a canal, river, brook, or marshy land?			
General Observations			

EXTRACTS FROM REPORTS OF CHRISTIAN INSTRUCTION SOCIETIES. *(Note, page 67.)*

Mosley-street Christian Instruction Society.

"ITS members agreed to consider a certain section of the Town, adjacent to the Chapel, as the field of their labour, and to visit periodically all the abodes of the poor within the limits so marked out, for the purpose of conversing with the inmates on the great truths of the gospel, lending them tracts and books on those momentous subjects, and inducing them to attend public worship, and to live themselves, and train up their children, as immortal beings. From that time to the present about forty individuals have followed out this undertaking within a district of which Market-street, Mosley-street, and Deansgate, on the South side, as far as Bootle-street, have constituted the boundaries. At the commencement of the present year, returns were made, from which the following facts were ascertained. The dwellings visited by the Society were about 350, containing nearly 600 families, which consisted of about 1800 *resident* members. In those families there were, children under ten years of age, 453; children sent to Day Schools, 149; children sent to Sunday Schools only, 240: children old enough for school but not sent, 93. There were, of families possessing bibles, 327; of families in which the adults did not regularly neglect public worship, only 150; of Catholic families, 60; of families the heads of which were *avowed* infidels, 5. To make the description of the Society's district answerable to the impressions of it on the minds of the visitors, there would have to be added, to these facts, details of drunkenness and sabbath-breaking, of vice and misery, of the complete negation of moral and religious sentiment, of flagrant vice, and shameless profligacy, of squalid poverty, of wasting sickness, and of hopeless death. When the visitors attained some extensive knowledge of the domestic circumstances and spiritual wants of the people whom they had taken under their charge, they became desirous to join, to their own agency, that of one who might give his whole time to such cases as were perpetually demanding more attention than they could possibly pay; cases of protracted illness, of approaching death, and of awakened inquiry, &c. For this office they selected a member of the church, Mr. Robinson, who has since devoted himself with the utmost diligence to the labours of his honourable, but arduous and extremely self-denying, vocation. Two preaching stations have been established; one in Queen-street, Deansgate, and one in Gee's Buildings, near Lloyd-street. Both are occupied on Sunday Evening; Mr. Robinson being engaged at one place, while private members of the church most kindly and acceptably supply the other."

London Christian Instruction Society.

"Its design is, irrespective of the particular denominations of Christians, to advance evangelical Religion amongst the inhabitants of the Metropolis and its Vicinity, by promoting the observance of the Sunday—the preaching of the Gospel—the establishment of Prayer Meetings and Sunday Schools—the circulation of Religious Tracts, accompanied with systematic visitation—and by the establishment of gratuitous Circulating Libraries—with every other legitimate method which the Committee may from time to time approve, for the accomplishment of the great object contemplated by the Society. To facilitate the operations of the Society, the Metropolis is divided, by the establishment of Associations, into districts, to each of which is appointed a Superintendent, with the approbation of the Committee, who presides over the proceedings of the Society in the District to which he belongs, and reports to the Committee, at their conference with the whole body of the Superintendents, the state of the District committed to his care. At the present time there are sixty-five Associations, which engage the benevolent attention of 1173 gratuitous visitors, who have, during the past year, visited 31,591 families, being an increase of 4677 families since the last Report. So that, by this agency alone, religious tracts and books are now placed within the reach of at least 150,000 individuals. Through the benevolent efforts of the Visitors during 1830, 1260 cases of extreme distress were relieved, 617 copies of the Sacred Scriptures were brought into circulation, and 2303 children were sent to the various Sabbath Schools, and more than 1200 individuals were induced to attend public worship. Many zealous Visitors have included within their spheres of benevolence, the hospitals, workhouses, police stations, and manufactories, that are found in their respective neighbourhoods. Connected with the numerous Associations are *ninety-three stations* for reading the Scriptures, exhortation, and prayer. These meetings are usually held in the apartments of the poor, who appear gratified with the opportunity of showing their respect for the Visitors by lending their abodes for such a purpose. At various stations not less than 200 sermons were preached to congregations, varying from 100 to 1000 persons."

Greenock City Mission.—"This society is engaged, 1st, In visiting the lower classes in their own houses; 2d, In collecting into one house individuals living in the same neighbourhood, for the purpose of reading and expounding the Scriptures; and 3d, In an investigation into the state of the community generally. From this investigation, it appears that Greenock contains 6,200 families, and 26,500 inhabitants, of whom 8,360 are below 12 years of age: 4,370 are betwixt 12 and 20: 13,970 are above 20 years. About 3000 children attend day schools, therefore there must be nearly 2000 betwixt 6 and 14 years of age, who do not attend school. It is not the business of the Directors to propose a remedy for this apparent neglect of education, but it certainly suggests the propriety of exertions being made, to have parish schools established in Greenock, being the *legal* means of affording cheap education to all classes. The number attending Sabbath evening schools is nearly 2,000, and there being about 5,000 youths in Greenock, betwixt 7 and 16 years of age, it follows that 3,000 receive no Sabbath school instruction. And allowing liberally for those whose parents instruct them at home, a number will still remain, sufficiently great, to show the necessity of more vigorous efforts to afford the means of religious instruction to the young. As far as could be ascertained, there are 500 individuals, chiefly grown up, who cannot read. The Directors particularly call attention to the subject of church accommodation and church attendance, information in regard to which is next in order. The number of sittings said to be taken in churches is 8,850, being only at the rate of two-thirds of a sitting to each person above 20 years of age—of course, one-third or 4,621 persons above 20 years, have no sittings in any church, and there is *no* provision at all for those *below* 20. It must be allowed that in a Christian community, every individual above 12 or 14 years of age ought to have a sitting in church, so that nine thousand in Greenock, above 14 years of age, are without sittings in any church. But, in fact, there is little more than church accommodation in town, for the number of sittings said to be taken, and several of the churches are not full; it follows therefore, that not nearly one half of the population above 12 years, attend church on any one Sabbath!! About 3,100 families state they belong to the Established Churches, 1,500 families are Dissenters, and 360 families are Catholics; nearly 1,200 families could not distinctly tell to what church they belonged!! Seven thousand two hundred persons are communicants, being only one half of the population above 20 years of age! Surely such a statement as this needs no comment, and the Directors merely draw from it a pressing argument for increased exertions to support this Society, whose object is to attend to those at home, who either cannot or will not come to the house of God. It is remarkable that there are no fewer than 1,450 widows who keep house, being betwixt a fourth and fifth of the whole number of householders. The number of paupers, or those who enjoy *regular* assistance from the parish funds, is about one thousand. It is unnecessary to state the number of families in want of Bibles, the Greenock Bible Society and Association, having kindly offered to supply any deficiency of this kind."

Glasgow City Mission.—"The object of the Mission is 'To promote the Religious Interests of the Poor of Glasgow and its vicinity.' It enacts that the Agents of the Society be chosen from all denominations of professing Christians: that they be men of approved piety, prudence, and zeal; and who, by their acquirements, especially in Divinity, may appear fitted for the duties of the agency: that the Agents occupy themselves, at least four hours daily, in the service of the society, excepting Saturday, which is allowed them for study; that they select such hours of call as will best suit the convenience of the people; and that no calls be made *at the hour of dinner:* that preaching-stations be appointed in the districts visited by the Agents, to which the poor shall be invited: and that the co-operation of ordained ministers and preachers of the Gospel be solicited to maintain worship at the said stations, &c. Lastly, that no Agent be required to act contrary to the laws prescribed to him, by that body of Christians with which he is connected. Of the twenty Agents employed in 1828, six were members of the Church of Scotland; ten, seceders, of the various sects; two Independents; one, a Reformed Presbyterian; and one, a Baptist.

"The printed 'Instructions to the Agents' are liberal and judicious; but they are too long to admit of being inserted. Every Agent has his own allotted district. He is required to keep a schedule, in which he enters the number of hours employed in the service of the society, and the number of families visited each day. He is also required to keep a regular journal or diary for the inspection of the Directors. An idea of the work done by the Agents, may be formed from the statement, that in the month of October, 1828, when only 16 Agents were in employment, *four thousand and seventy families* were visited in the ordinary course of visitation. *Two hundred and eighty-eight* sick and dying had special visits paid to them; 239 meetings were held, attended by as many as 2514 poor; chiefly of such a class as otherwise might not have heard the Gospel. The number of families, the subjects of regular visitation, in 1828, was about *twelve thousand.* These devoted Agents read and expound the Holy Scriptures to the poor, and converse with them on every topic connected with their own religious instruction, and that of their children. They supply them with books and tracts. They enlist their children as scholars in the various Sunday Schools, which happily are to be found in every neighbourhood. In cases of extreme want and destitution, they are also often the means of obtaining pecuniary help, through the benevolence of opulent individuals, to whom they consider it a part of their duty to make such cases known."

TABLE of the number of Irish cases without Settlements, and of all cases that have obtained Settlements, and hence denominated English, (whether English or Irish,) which received Parochial Relief in the Township of Manchester, in the four winter months of the years* 1827-8, 1828-9, 1829-30, 1830-31, *and of the sums thus expended.

*No. 1.	NEWTOWN.					ANCOATS.					CENTRAL.					PORTLAND STREET.				
	No. of Cases.		*Amount pd.*			*No. of Cases.*		*Amount pd.*			*No. of Cases.*		*Amount pd.*			*No. of Cases.*		*Amount pd.*		
			L.	*s.*	*d.*			*L.*	*s.*	*d.*			*L.*	*s.*	*d.*			*L.*	*s.*	*d.*
1827 and 1828.																				
November.	English	1456	208	18	3	English	1694	207	17	0	English	1818	245	13	0	English	1670	226	3	6
	Irish	369	54	10	6	Irish	348	38	0	6	Irish					Irish				
December.	English	1534	204	12	0	English	1708	209	11	6	English	1874	246	10	6	English	1732	229	9	0
	Irish	396	52	17	6	Irish	379	41	10	6	Irish					Irish				
January.	English	1561	213	1	2	English	1674	205	8	0	English	1911	262	2	6	English	1738	237	9	0
	Irish	400	54	14	6	Irish	386	42	3	6	Irish	195	19	19	0	Irish	133	12	17	0
February.	English	1508	210	2	6	English	1625	193	9	0	English	1819	232	8	6	English	1724	223	19	0
	Irish	394	51	14	0	Irish	369	39	10	0	Irish	171	16	19	6	Irish	131	13	1	6
1828 and 1829.		7618	1050	10	5		8183	977	10	0		7788	1023	13	0		7128	932	19	0
November.	English	1291	153	9	6	English	1620	191	1	6	English	1684	208	7	9½	English	1689	205	18	0
	Irish	309	34	0	6	Irish	488	56	12	0	Irish	122	12	5	0	Irish	144	14	10	0
December.	English	1339	159	7	6	English	1701	207	18	6	English	1784	216	17	0	English	1737	211	8	0
	Irish	342	37	2	0	Irish	507	57	4	6	Irish	134	15	7	0	Irish	130	15	5	6
January.	English	1347	161	8	0	English	1836	221	8	0	English	1847	231	0	3	English	1748	219	19	6
	Irish	365	39	7	0	Irish	547	62	9	0	Irish	133	15	6	3	Irish	147	15	8	0
February.	English	1457	179	1	0	English	2001	244	4	0	English	1847	236	4	0	English	1800	227	6	0
	Irish	474	55	7	6	Irish	613	72	4	6	Irish	143	15	9	6	Irish	156	16	4	6
1829 and 1830.		6924	819	3	0		9313	1113	2	0		7694	950	16	9½		7551	925	19	6
November.	English	2053	292	2	1	English	2069	245	9	6	English	2278	329	5	6	English	2030	269	0	0
	Irish	930	114	19	6	Irish	639	68	5	6	Irish	166	19	19	0	Irish	228	22	6	0
December.	English	1997	285	14	6	English	1960	228	5	0	English	2346	320	13	3	English	2121	282	5	0
	Irish	985	122	3	4	Irish	640	65	5	0	Irish	168	19	14	6	Irish	259	24	2	6
January.	English	1931	267	15	2	English	1934	231	14	1½	English	2481	363	6	5	English	2150	278	19	6
	Irish	961	127	18	10	Irish	694	74	5	7½	Irish	198	23	8	6	Irish	320	28	16	0
February.	English	2042	290	11	11	English	2059	245	9	11	English	2563	365	9	3	English	2290	307	2	9
	Irish	1035	137	8	9	Irish	717	80	6	0	Irish	210	25	18	0	Irish	379	34	9	6
1830 and 1831.		11934	1638	14	1		10712	1239	0	8		10410	1467	14	5		9777	1247	1	3
November.	English	2065	322	1	6	English	2210	278	1	6½	English	2395	321	15	1	English	1765	202	5	6
	Irish	925	125	8	6	Irish	925	125	8	6	Irish	204	24	9	6	Irish	230	23	1	6
December.	English	2374	360	9	5	English	2333	314	5	10	English	2597	351	3	9½	English	1864	225	12	8
	Irish	1128	157	17	6	Irish	978	107	5	0	Irish	233	30	10	2	Irish	289	29	1	6
January.	English	2477	428	14	4	English	2328	336	3	8½	English	2673	377	8	10	English	1984	242	12	10½
	Irish	1022	146	4	6	Irish	994	107	9	0	Irish	243	32	10	0	Irish	304	30	17	0
February.	English	2213	335	2	6	English	2201	278	7	8	English	2549	348	1	6	English	1967	231	8	0
	Irish	976	133	3	3	Irish	921	96	8	0	Irish	229	29	0	6	Irish	291	30	19	6
		13180	2009	1	6		12890	1643	9	3		11123	1514	19	4½		8694	1015	18	6½

PAROCHIAL RELIEF *administered in eight months of the year* 1831, *in the TOWNSHIP of MANCHESTER.*

*No. 2.	NEWTOWN.					ANCOATS.					CENTRAL.					PORTLAND STREET.				
1831.	*No. of Cases.*		*Amount paid.*			*No. of Cases.*		*Amount paid.*			*No. of Cases.*		*Amount paid.*			*No. of Cases.*		*Amount paid.*		
			£.	s.	d.			£.	s.	d.			£.	s.	d.			£.	s.	d.
March.	English	2037	285	12	8	English	1943	250	19	6	English	2430	334	19	4	English	1764	199	3	10
	Irish	1099	138	2	4	Irish	804	86	6	6	Irish	226	28	8	6	Irish	236	25	0	6
April.	English	2022	317	3	4½	English	1917	264	8	6	English	2879	332	4	0½	English	1769	213	5	0
	Irish	984	127	16	9	Irish	806	85	15	0	Irish	202	23	18	2	Irish	230	25	3	0
May.	English	1931	293	16	6	English	1961	254	7	6	English	2285	314	6	9½	English	1735	204	14	2½
	Irish	902	116	11	6	Irish	841	88	14	0	Irish	180	21	12	2	Irish	214	21	9	0
June.	English	1968	286	6	8	English	1980	249	4	6	English	2380	327	15	10	English	1782	207	2	6
	Irish	911	117	7	6	Irish	882	94	1	0	Irish	207	24	3	0	Irish	217	21	13	6
		11854	1682	17	3½		11134	1373	16	6		10289	1403	7	10		7947	917	11	6½
July.	English	1986	306	14	10½	English	1969	275	18	6	English	2378	323	15	0	English	1730	218	5	8
	Irish	888	117	7	2	Irish	856	92	12	6	Irish	199	25	1	0	Irish	220	24	10	7½
August.	English	1987	291	8	11½	English	2024	271	1	9	English	2324	305	15	8	English	1687	205	8	6
	Irish	856	115	19	10	Irish	813	83	10	6	Irish	175	21	6	6	Irish	227	24	12	0
Septemb.	English	2086	294	3	11	English	2023	274	18	4½	English	2284	307	18	6	English	1754	201	12	6
	Irish	856	110	0	6	Irish	823	85	1	0	Irish	152	16	19	0	Irish	205	20	3	6
October.	English	1937	289	10	10	English	2091	258	19	2	English	2301	312	10	2	English	1732	179	7	6
	Irish	809	106	1	9	Irish	788	80	12	0	Irish	169	19	4	2	Irish	211	20	17	0
		11405	1631	7	10		11387	1422	19	9½		9982	1332	10	0		7766	894	7	3½

For Product Safety Concerns and Information please contact our EU
representative GPSR@taylorandfrancis.com
Taylor & Francis Verlag GmbH, Kaufingerstraße 24, 80331 München, Germany

www.ingramcontent.com/pod-product-compliance
Lightning Source LLC
LaVergne TN
LVHW021112300926
849160LV00009B/702
* 9 7 8 0 3 6 7 1 4 9 8 5 7 *